NEW

JO AVERY

Patchwork & Quilting *basics*

A Handbook for Beginners • 12 Projects to Get You Started

stashBOOKS.

an imprint of C&T Publishing

Text copyright © 2020 by Jo Avery

Photography and artwork copyright © 2020 by C&T Publishing, Inc.

PUBLISHER: Amy Barrett-Daffin

CREATIVE DIRECTOR: Gailen Runge

ACQUISITIONS EDITOR: Roxane Cerda

MANAGING EDITOR: Liz Aneloski

EDITOR: Kathryn Patterson

TECHNICAL EDITOR: Helen Frost

COVER/BOOK DESIGNER: April Mostek

PRODUCTION COORDINATOR: Zinnia Heinzmann

PRODUCTION EDITOR: Jennifer Warren

ILLUSTRATOR: Aliza Shalit

PHOTO ASSISTANT: Rachel Holmes

LIFESTYLE PHOTOGRAPHY by Kelly Burgoyne of C&T Publishing, Inc.;
SUBJECTS AND INSTRUCTIONAL PHOTOGRAPHY by Diane Pedersen

Published by Stash Books, an imprint of C&T Publishing, Inc., P.O. Box 1456,
Lafayette, CA 94549

Library of Congress Cataloging-in-Publication Data

Names: Avery, Jo, 1966 author.

Title: New patchwork & quilting basics : a handbook for beginners - 12 projects to get you
started / Jo Avery.

Description: Lafayette, CA : C&T Publishing, Inc., [2020]

Identifiers: LCCN 2019019719 | ISBN 9781617458484 (softcover)

Subjects: LCSH: Quilting--Patterns. | Patchwork--Patterns. | Art quilts.

Classification: LCC TT835 .A96 2020 | DDC 746.46/041--dc23

LC record available at https://lccn.loc.gov/2019019719

Printed in the USA

10 9 8 7 6 5 4 3

Dedication

For the three men in my life: Jonathan, Felix, and Jacob.
Thanks for putting up with the endless quilt chat.

Acknowledgments

I'd like to thank the following people for helping me achieve this long-held ambition to write a quilt book:

My sister, Jane Read, who patiently taught me to sew when I was six years old and has been my best sewing pal ever since. I owe this all to you, Jane!

Jane Wilson, my girl Friday, you are a brick and a star.

Lisi Brydon, my absolute BFF.

Karen Lewis, my Thread House partner in crime, thank you for always being there with support and advice.

Lynne Goldsworthy, my quilting hero, who led us all from the start.

Sarah Ashford, my quilting little sis, thanks for all your enthusiasm.

Dolores Goodson, my loudest and most loyal cheerleader.

Pam Fallon-Cousins, my fellow chainee and QuiltCon travel consultant.

Jenny Fox-Proverbs, for giving me my first chance to shine.

Liz Taylor and all the team at Immediate Media, for giving me so much support and encouragement.

Ali Myer, for helping me get started on this project.

Kelly Orr and Tatyana Duffie, thank you for your talented and creative quilting abilities.

Ali Watt, for the friendship, Friday chats, and karaoke.

Sarah Roberts, for all those years we spent together and your unswerving belief in me.

All my pals at the Edinburgh MQG and all my lovely customers at myBearpaw.

Thanks also to the following companies for their help with thread, fabric, and batting:

Aurifil, Hobbs, Moda Fabrics + Supplies, Riley Blake Designs, and Robert Kaufman Fabrics.

contents

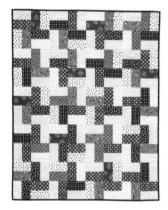
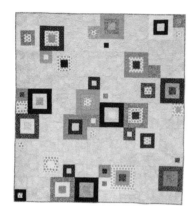
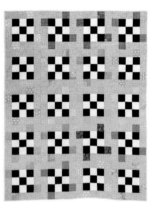

SKILL BUILDING 65

MIX AND MATCH 85

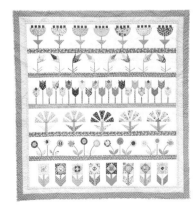

Foreword

Quilting is a special pastime and one that you never really get to the end of. It's so much more than cutting up fabric and sewing it together again. It's a lifetime passion full of creativity, nostalgia, and humanity. Quilters are part of a generous and special community of makers, whether that be in real-life local groups or virtual ones that span the globe. They spend any available time turning fabric into beautiful pieces of craft that also comfort and inspire—and they like to be together when they are doing it to share their love and experience.

I began my quilting journey at 10 years old, when my big sister, Jane, taught me to sew patchwork hexagons. When I found myself at 21 and with my own home for the first time, I naturally began another hexagon quilt. I was instinctively nesting and creating something practical and satisfying with my own hands. It was the first of many quilts I would make over the next 30 years. A decade ago, I began to teach the art of patchwork and quilting, and found a new joy in spreading the message and welcoming new members to our "cult." But time and space mean I can only teach 8 new quilters at a time. When I was offered the opportunity to write a book for beginner quilters, I jumped at it. At last, a way to create not just handfuls of new quilters but potentially thousands!

I hope the pages that follow will inspire you to join us and become a quilter, too!

Introduction

In the following pages, I plan to offer as complete and concise a quilt course as possible in the space available. This a basics book with instructions for a complete beginner to the craft, but I wanted it to be more than a selection of quick, simple quilts. I want my students to feel that they have gained certain skills from making each quilt. They can then build on these by moving on to the next quilt and tackling the next set of techniques with confidence.

We will begin with the simplest crib quilt and build from there through strips, squares, and triangles to give us a good grounding in piecing. We will then branch out into different and important techniques such as curves, appliqué, and foundation paper piecing. There are a variety of smaller projects mixed in amongst the quilts, enabling you to give these new skills a try before committing too much time. In the last part of the book, we will mix all those techniques together to make three intermediate quilts. I have every confidence that by working through the previous projects you will be more than capable of making these more ambitious designs.

In this book, I hope to convey my own personal philosophy and thoughts about quilting. But there are many different views on the right and wrong ways to tackle various aspects of our craft, and I would encourage beginners to learn from as wide a pool of quilters as possible before finding the methods that suit them.

I believe that making a quilt is as much about the journey as the destination. Try not to get too impatient about the amount of time some of the stages take but instead focus on the actual process and the enjoyment and satisfaction it gives. When your quilt is finally complete—no matter how long it has taken—you will be able to bask in the glow of a job well done before grabbing your fabric and starting the next one!

Getting Started

what is a quilt?

I start each beginner's class in my studio by describing the difference between *patchwork* and *quilting*, something that is not always clearly understood. *Patchwork* is the act of sewing pieces of fabric together to make a new piece of fabric. *Quilting* is the act of stitching through three layers of material—a top, a backing, and a middle layer of (usually, but not exclusively) batting. It is only a quilt once these three layers have been stitched together. You can make a piece of patchwork and back it with fabric and it will be a *patchwork throw*, but not a quilt. Or you can sandwich batting between two whole pieces of fabric and stitch them together; you would have a quilt but not a *patchwork* quilt.

There are many other technical terms that quilters use to describe their processes, and we will begin with the following glossary to help you as you move through the book.

quilting terms and abbreviations

Basting: Also known as *layering up*, this describes the method used to secure the three quilt layers together prior to the quilting process.

Batting: This is the middle layer of the quilt, also known as *wadding*. It is most commonly made from cotton or a cotton/polyester mix; however, other materials such as wool, bamboo, and silk are also available. My preferred choice is Hobbs' Tuscany Cotton Wool Batting, a blended mix of 80% cotton and 20% wool. I would always advise against using 100% polyester batting if possible.

Binding: A strip of fabric sewn around the edge of a quilt to finish it

Blocks: A square (usually) of fabric made up of patchwork pieces. Blocks are sewn together to make a quilt top.

Borders: Strips of fabric that frame your quilt top, adding definition and increasing size

Cornerstones: Squares placed at the corners of blocks in the sashing and borders

Fat quarter: An 18″ × 20″–22″ cut of fabric

FPP: Abbreviation for *foundation paper piecing*

Fussy cutting: To identify and cut a particular motif from a piece of fabric

HST: Abbreviation for *half-square triangles*

Low-volume fabric: Subtle, neutral fabrics that still contain a pattern

Medallion quilt: A quilt design that starts from the center and works out, and where most borders contain patchwork elements

On point: A way of placing your patchwork blocks in your quilt top so that they appear as diamonds rather than squares

Piecing: Sewing the pieces of patchwork fabric together, either by hand or machine

QST: Abbreviation for *quarter-square triangles*

Quilting: Stitching the three layers together, either by hand or machine

Quilt top: The top layer of the quilt; this can be either patchwork or just plain fabric (wholecloth).

Sampler quilt: A quilt where each of the blocks is a different design and technique

Sashing: A lattice of strips sewn between blocks

WOF: Abbreviation for *width of fabric*

toolbox

Quilters tend to love tools and gadgets, and there are a lot available. Here are my essential items.

Sewing Machine and Feet

The three crucial feet for quilting are a ¼″ foot, a walking foot, and a free-motion quilting (FMQ) foot. The ¼″ foot comes with or without a flange on the side for guiding the fabric. The ones with guides are easier for beginners but I find those without are better for improving your accuracy. A walking foot is extremely helpful for straight-line quilting, and the FMQ foot is essential for free-motion quilting.

Rotary Cutter

There are so many from which to choose, but I prefer a small and light 28 mm cutter for everyday use. The self-closing versions are good for beginners. Don't forget to buy spare blades and use them!

Self-Healing Mat

The 12″ × 18″ mats are perfect to begin with and small enough to take to workshops. Upgrade to 18″ × 24″ (or larger) for home use when you can.

Ruler

I have at least seven different sizes and use them all daily. A 6½″ × 12½″ (or 6″ × 12″) ruler is a good starting point, but as you get going you should also invest in a 6½″ × 24½″ (or 6″ × 24″) and a 12½″ square ruler.

Pins

A good-quality sharp pin is so important. Glass-head pins won't melt when you iron over them and flower-head pins lie nice and flat, but steel dressmaking pins work just as well. I love Clover appliqué pins for small hand-sewing projects because they don't catch on your threads as you are sewing.

Scissors

Almost all your fabric will be cut with your rotary cutter, so it is important to have scissors that are easy to handle rather than heavy-duty dressmaking shears. You will need scissors for cutting out pattern pieces and delicate snipping. I like my medium-sized Fiskars for most jobs, along with a tiny pair of embroidery snips for hand sewing. Keep a pair of large scissors just for cutting your batting, as this job tends to blunt them.

Seam Ripper

A good, sharp seam ripper is as important as good, sharp scissors. Don't buy the cheapest, and replace them regularly—their blades become blunt like all sharp tools.

Needles

For my sewing machine, I use any brand in size 80 or 90 and change my needle after each quilt. For hand sewing, I am much fussier. For appliqué, I use a straw milliners size 10, and for hand quilting with 12-weight thread, I use a sharps size 5. My favorite brands are Milward and Tulip. I also like easy-threading needles for threading my ends in after quilting.

Thimble

A thimble on the middle finger of your right hand is essential for hand quilting. If you don't use one, you will very soon have an actual hole in the side of that finger, which will hurt! Many people struggle with metal thimbles, but there are so many options on the market now, from silicone to leather, that there is sure to be one that works for you. My favorite is a Clover Leather Thimble.

Add-A-Quarter Ruler

This clever ruler has been designed especially for FPP. It has a lip along one edge that fits snuggly over the seam allowance so you can accurately trim a ¼″ from your sewn line.

Hera Marker

I am always worried about using any sort of pen to mark lines on my quilts. Even when I have successfully tested the removability of various pens, I still prefer using my Clover Hera Marker for drawing my quilting lines. This creasing tool leaves a sharp enough line to follow but nothing that needs to be removed later.

Binding Clips

What did we do before these came along? They are my "desert island" notion and are useful for so many applications. Binding clips are much easier than pins for holding bulky layers together, such as binding, and are invaluable for zippers and bag making.

Flatter Spray

This spray, made by Soak, works like a starch, but I feel it makes fabric even flatter. It can be used prior to pressing when prepping fabric for appliqué, and some people use it before cutting their fabric. It is also very helpful with stubbornly bulky seams or where seams have been pressed in the wrong direction and need to be corrected.

Curved Safety Pins

These are used during quilt basting; the curved edge makes it easier to get them through the three quilt layers.

Odif 505 Spray

This temporary spray adhesive has revolutionized my basting procedure. I always have a can at home.

Thread

My favorite thread is by Aurifil; it's simply the best cotton thread available for patchwork and quilting. I use the 50-weight thread for all my piecing and machine quilting, the 80-weight thread for hand appliqué, and the 12-weight thread for hand quilting and embroidery.

---

fabric

Let's face it—the reason you want to make a quilt is most likely because of fabric. My view is that people start quilting so that they can justify buying that gorgeous fabric they've seen, and they keep making quilts so that they can buy more and more fabric!

This is a long way from the "make do and mend" history of our craft, when thrifty quilters reused every precious scrap of cloth until it literally fell apart. Today we luxuriate in a wealth of craft fabrics produced just for our hobby. I would love to encourage beginner sewists to continue to

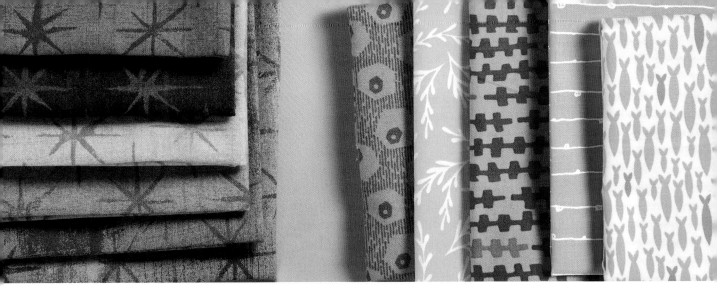

recycle and reuse old fabrics—but maybe not for the first few quilts. It is so much easier to learn to quilt with new, stable, similar-weight cotton fabric than with old clothes of differing weights and made from different materials.

To begin with, buy good-quality cotton fabric from reputable manufacturers. If fabric is very inexpensive there will be a reason for it. You are making heirlooms here, so don't skimp on your materials. Avoid stretchy or shiny fabrics and fabrics with a pile until you are more experienced.

Prewashing

Good-quality quilting cotton does not need to be prewashed. You may still want to do this with very dark colors and with fabrics that are a linen/cotton mix. I would also prewash any recycled or inherited fabrics.

Choosing Fabrics

This is a subject for a whole book in itself and will become easier with experience, but to begin with, buy fabrics you like and don't worry too much about making them coordinate. Antique patch-work quilts had all sorts thrown in, which is part of their charm.

If you struggle with decision-making or visualization, then trust a fabric designer to do the work for you. They produce fabric lines with a mixture of blenders and larger prints in a range of colors that all work together. Favorite designers who do this particularly well include Carolyn Friedlander, Jennifer Paganelli, and Valori Wells.

My main piece of advice when choosing fabric for a project is to keep color tone in mind. *Tone* is the amount of gray in each color. Colors have a pure hue and can become *tints* by adding white or *shades* by adding black. By adding different amounts of gray, colors become a range of tones. A fresh, vibrant fabric will have very little gray, whereas a muted, grungy fabric will have a lot. You can mix many different colors together in your quilts and it will still be harmonious as long as they remain a similar tone.

Building a Stash

It's important to start building your stash early on. The idea that you can buy fabric for one project at a time and use it all up is fiction. You will always have some left and will need to buy new fabric to use with this. I would advise buying useful and beautiful fabric that makes you happy. You don't have a fabric addiction; you are curating a fabric collection!

cutting, piecing, and pressing

As you progress along your quilting journey, the word *accuracy* will start to make more frequent appearances. By cutting the fabric accurately and piecing it accurately, we hope to achieve a good result, with each block ending up the same size and our points matching. Accuracy is a constant ideal for a quilter; even the most experienced will still strive for more. To begin with, we will concentrate on enough to get you started without scaring you and bamboozling you with too much information. As you gain experience and practice, your accuracy will naturally improve and you can then go on to learn the many tweaks to techniques that will give your piecing that extra edge.

Cutting

For quilters, the rotary cutter, self-healing mat, and acrylic ruler enjoy a similar stature to the wheel as regards important inventions. Everything changed when they came along in the 1980s: Fabric could now be cut accurately and with speed. These three items work together, and it is important that the grid on your ruler matches the grid on your mat. Always press your fabric before you begin cutting.

Mat and Ruler Combined

The simplest way to begin cutting a strip of fabric is to use the mat and ruler together. Fold the fabric in two, right sides out, and align the folded edge with a horizontal line on the mat, with the right-hand edges of the fabric just over one of the vertical lines. Align the vertical lines on your ruler with the vertical lines on the mat below, and cut along the vertical line closest to the right-hand edge of the fabric. This will give you a straight edge to work from.

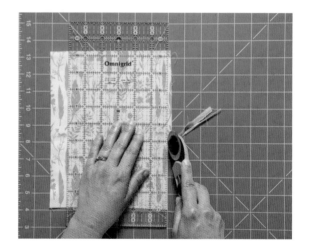

Move the ruler along the number of inches required and make a second cut to give you a strip. Continue to move your ruler to the left to cut more strips. *Note:* Use the opposite edges if you are left-handed.

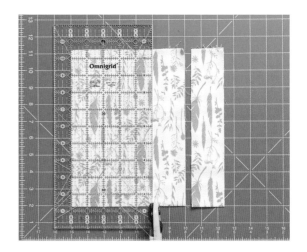

Ruler Only

As you become more accustomed to using your mat and ruler, try this next method. It is a little more accurate and will make your mat last longer. Though the mats are self-healing, repeated cutting on the same lines will eventually wear through the mat and may blunt your cutter.

Fold the fabric in two, right sides out, and place on your mat. Place the ruler over the left side of the fabric, aligning the folded edge with a horizontal line on the ruler. Cut along a vertical line a little over the required width of strip.

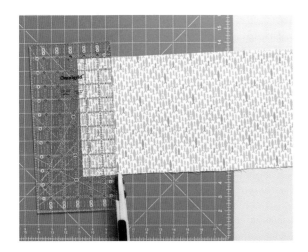

Carefully flip the strip over and align the ruler again with the fold line. Cut the strip by aligning the vertical line for the required width of strip with the recently cut edge. Move the ruler over the fabric to cut more strips. *Note:* Use the opposite edges if you are left-handed.

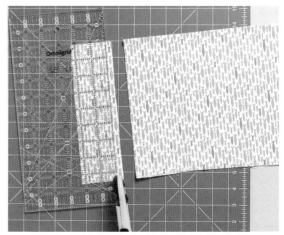

To cut squares or other shapes from your strips, simply align the cut edges of your strip either with the lines on the mat and ruler combined or with the ruler alone. You can stack up to 4 layers of fabric together to speedily cut pieces.

Cutting an Individual Square

If only a couple of squares are needed from a particular fabric, place the corner of the ruler over one corner of the fabric, slightly over the required size of square, and cut around the two edges of the ruler.

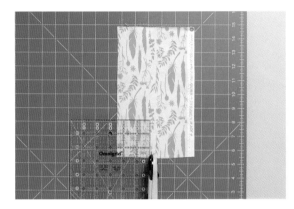

Turn the square a full 90° and align the cut edges with the exact size of square required. Cut along the two ruler sides to trim away excess. This method can also be used when fussy cutting a particular motif from a fabric.

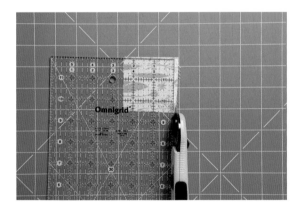

Using Your Cutter Safely—5 Cardinal Rules

1. Keep your cutter closed when not using it. It is extremely important to close the rotary cutter's safety shield *every time* you lay it down. Get into this habit early on and stick to it.

2. Always cut away from your body. The rotary cutter should always roll away from you. Never attempt to cut backwards toward yourself. If the cutter hasn't gone through all the layers, go back to the start and recut away from you. Cutting with a sawing action will damage the edges of your fabric.

3. Keep your fingers away from the ruler's edge. Right-handed quilters must hold the ruler steady with the left hand while cutting down the right edge of the ruler. Left-handed quilters will reverse the process. Try to keep an equal pressure between your ruler in one hand and your cutter in the other.

4. Always cut standing up. Don't attempt to rotary cut with a regular cutter while sitting down. You can't hold the ruler or the cutter correctly in that position.

5. Change your blade regularly. A rotary cutter should cut through 4 layers of fabric with ease; it should not be a huge effort. If you are continually repeating the same cut, your blade needs changing. Also keep pins away from your mat at all times. There is nothing worse than changing your blade and then running over a pin and immediately nicking it in one spot!

Thoughts on Inches Versus Centimeters

As a unit of length, the inch is simply perfect for patchwork, and I would strongly recommend using it even if you live in a place where metric predominates. You will soon learn that math and arithmetic are key to quilting, and the larger size of the inch makes these much easier on your brain. Blocks are sized at predominantly 6″, 9″, and 12″ and are made up of units of 2″, 3″, and 4″. It is so much easier to work out the simple arithmetic with these than if you are using numbers such as 17 and 23. You will also find that most patterns and notions are written in inches, and translating to centimeters often gives bad results.

Piecing

Patchwork is a great way to get plenty of easy practice at machine sewing, as it involves little more than sewing a straight line.

It is important to sew your fabric pieces together with a consistent seam, and the standard seam for patchwork is a ¼″. This is one of the smallest seams you will be asked to sew, and if you are new to machine sewing, it may be challenging. Using a ¼″ foot with a guide is the most accurate way to achieve it. Until you become practiced at piecing, regularly check your seam allowances from the back to make sure they are consistent and not getting too big or too small. *All seam allowances in this book are ¼″ unless otherwise stated.*

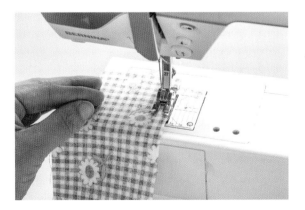

Locking Seams

At the beginning and ending of every seam, you should reverse your stitches to lock the seams. This should become an automatic action, a quick pulse of reverse stitches as you start and stop sewing each seam. It is integral to the longevity of your quilt that all the many seams you stitch are locked at either end. Some machines offer an automatic lockstitch option.

Stitch Length

Your stitch length for basic piecing should be between 2.0 mm and 2.5 mm. If you are stitching a set of strips that will then be cut into sections (meaning there will be unlocked seams), reduce your stitch length to 1.8 mm–2.0 mm.

tip || **Test It Out**

When working on a quilt pattern, always make at least one block as a test before cutting all your fabric—just in case!

Pressing

Pressing seams is one of those controversial areas of quiltmaking that can divide quilters. The question is whether seams should be pressed to one side or pressed open. I prefer to press my seams to one side for a few basic but important reasons:

1. It's quicker! Pressing seams open is fiddly and slow and can burn your fingers.

2. It's better for the integrity of your quilt. Once your seams are pressed safely to one side and stitched in place by quilting lines, those seam stitches are much safer than if the seams had been pressed open. Your thread is also less likely to be seen.

3. Nesting (as detailed on the next page) is the best way to get your points to match and is only possible when pressing to one side. As you get more practiced at piecing, you will learn to use your "pressed to one side" seams to anchor your long seams when sewing together pieced strips.

There are times when opening seams is appropriate, such as at the later stages of piecing a block when seams have become very bulky or when stitching strips together for borders and sashing, where open seams will help disguise joins.

As a general rule, you should press your seams toward dark fabric and away from light, and away from pieces with seams. Otherwise, I tend to press toward the side that the fabric is naturally leaning toward. Slight differences in fabric weight mean that lighter fabrics will always bend more easily than a heavier neighbor.

I would encourage you to try both methods of pressing to find the one that suits you best, as it is such a personal preference.

I prefer not to use steam when ironing, as this can stretch fabrics and interfere with accuracy. Instead, I like to use a spray starch.

Develop a good finger-pressing technique. Many seams do not need pressing until the block is finished. Finger-press (or nail press to be more accurate) on a hard surface from the right side, making sure your seams are flat. If you find this difficult, try one of the small pressing rollers that are designed for this job.

Nesting Seams

When joining pieced units together, press seams in opposite directions so that when you place the pieces together the seams "nest" where they intersect. Place pins at this intersection to keep them locked together as you sew. Open the pieces and press the seam to one side.

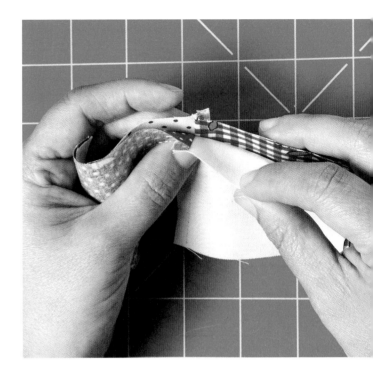

tip || **Match It Up!**

Sometimes getting points to match is particularly difficult due to fabrics shifting slightly as you sew your seam. Try beginning your seam just before the intersection. When you've finished sewing in one direction, return to the beginning of your seam and head in the opposite direction to complete.

Thoughts on Perfection

If you are an extreme perfectionist, then quilting may not be for you. Fabric is not a stable material like wood or metal, and fabric made in different factories from different parts of the world may not fit together as perfectly as you had hoped, despite all your best efforts at accuracy. But this is okay because you are a human being and not a robot, and you are making something unique by hand. It is not supposed to be uniform and bland. All those little idiosyncrasies and accidents are part of what makes a quilt a handmade piece of art.

If you are struggling, full of doubt, and about to rip out a seam that you think isn't perfect enough, then I would suggest that you stop and wait. Put that piece aside, move on to another area of your quilt, and leave any decisions about ripping until the last minute. We often get too close to our work, and all those tiny imperfections become magnified. When you move away and come back to it later, you will find it hard to spot the problem that was bothering you. If it stills bothers you on your return, then you have my permission to remove the stitches.

quilting

In many ways, this last stage of making a quilt can be the most challenging and technical of the whole process. But it should also take less time than making the top and is an integral part of quiltmaking. It is so much more than just securing the three layers together and, in my opinion, contains as much potential for creativity as the patchwork. I would encourage all of you to try and quilt your own quilts, no matter your level of experience. You can't really call yourself a quilter if you don't actually quilt!

Preparing to Quilt

Once you have finished piecing your patchwork top, give it a good pressing all over and remove any stray threads that make their way through the seams. This is also a good opportunity to check for and fix any issues such unsecured seams, puckers, or holes. Depending on the size of your quilt, you may need to piece a backing from lengths of fabric. If you don't want to bother with fiddly pattern matching, choose a solid or small overall print for the backing. Cut the length into equal pieces and remove selvages along the edges that will be seamed together. Pin then sew together using a ½″ seam. Press the seam open and give the whole piece a good pressing. Both your backing fabric and batting should be at least 4″ larger all around than your patchwork top.

Basting

There are three main ways to baste or layer up your quilt sandwich: pinning, spray basting, or thread basting. First you will need to find a large enough surface to spread out your layers, such as a hard floor or large table.

Method 1: Pinning

Place the backing down first, wrong side up, and use masking tape to secure it along each side. The fabric should be taut but not overstretched. Next place the batting on top, smoothing from the middle outward. Add the quilt top, right side up, and smooth it to make it as flat as possible. You can also press the whole thing again at this stage.

Use size 1 curved safety pins (large safety pins can leave holes in the fabric). Start pinning in the center, with pins 4″–8″ apart, and work outward. I find it's more efficient to insert the pins in an area and then close them afterward.

Method 2: Spray Basting

Prepare your 3 layers in a different order from the pinning method. Begin by taping the corners and the center of each edge of the batting to the floor, being careful not to over-stretch it. Lay your backing on top, right side up. Fold back one-half of the backing and spray the batting, following the instructions on the can of basting spray, before smoothing the backing back over the batting. You can use a wooden dowel or long ruler to help with this (or ask a friend to help with a corner!). If you encounter any ripples, simply peel back the backing and smooth again. Repeat with the other half of the backing. Flip the whole thing over, reattach the corner tape, and repeat with the top. You can also lightly press both sides once the layers are adhered. For extra security, attach safety pins around the outer edge.

Method 3: Thread Basting

I find thread basting works best for hand quilting. It is much more time consuming than the other methods but will hold layers securely for longer. I usually do this on a large table on top of an oilcloth tablecloth. This can be moved around if necessary without disturbing the layers. There is no need to attach your backing to the surface, as you will want to get your hand underneath the layers. Use a light-colored thread and cut the thread the width of the top. Lay the thread along the top and start sewing in the middle of the quilt with the middle of the long thread. Sew outwards in big basting (tacking) stitches, leaving a tail long enough to sew in the opposite direction when finished. Baste in lines 4″–8″ apart across both the width and the length so your tacking forms a grid pattern. For extra security, you can also tack diagonal lines. Baste around the outer edge.

Quilting

There are three main ways to quilt your quilt top: by hand, by machine using a walking foot, or by machine using free-motion quilting. I use all three methods, sometimes combining them together, as different quilt tops demand different treatments depending on the design and intended use. There are also plenty of professional longarm quilters that you can use for this stage. This service is especially useful if your quilt is particularly large or requires a special design.

Hand Quilting

Hand quilting can be an easy and less stressful way to finish a quilt for a beginner, and it doesn't need to take too long. A quilting stitch is a basic running stitch. Try to make the stitches the same size and same distance apart. You can buy special coated quilting thread that will give you a subtle effect. I prefer to use a 12-weight embroidery thread in a range of colors; the thicker thread means you can make your stitches a little larger. You should aim to have about 4″ between your quilting lines. As your quilt will be viewed from both sides, you will need to bury your knots at the start and finish of each thread. You can use a quilting hoop (like a large embroidery hoop) or a large frame for hand quilting, though neither are essential. I tend to use the patterns made by the block design for my hand quilting. For something more ambitious, there are quilting stencils and quilting pens and pencils available to mark your pattern (the marks from which can be removed later).

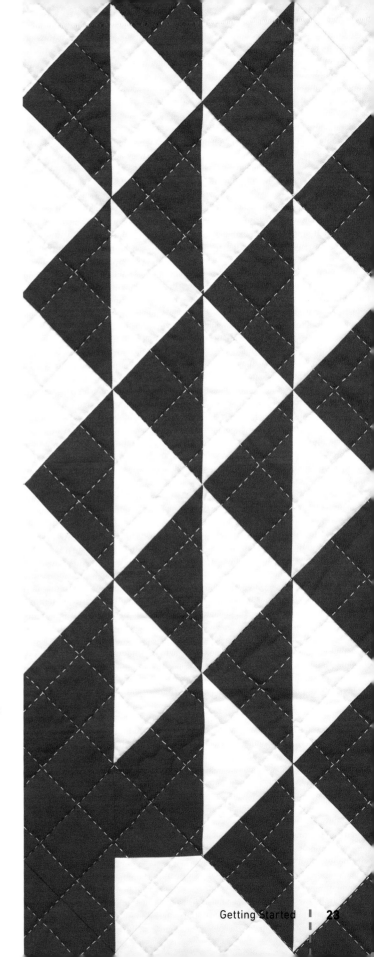

Machine Quilting with a Walking Foot

This is often called *straight-line quilting*, but you don't have to stitch only straight lines. You can also use wavy lines (as done in *Dancing Pandas Quilt*, page 40) or create continuous circles. You will need a walking-foot attachment specific to your machine make and model. A large stitch length looks more attractive. I use 3.5–4, but you can go up to 5 in size. It's best to stitch your lines in the same direction and from the center of one of the edges working outward. Roll the side of your quilt that is next to the machine throat and secure. An extension table and plenty of space around your sewing machine is essential for machine quilting. I also recommend using quilting gloves for both machine-quilting methods, as you will need more grip than you think for a full-size quilt.

Machine Quilting with Free-Motion Quilting

This is my favorite method of quilting and the most creatively rewarding, but it does take more practice than the others. It's like doodling or drawing, except your "pencil" (the needle) is fixed in place and you are moving your "paper" (the quilt) beneath it. You will need to drop your feed dogs or cover them with a darning plate (a card piece with a hole cut for the needle also works), and attach a free-motion or darning foot. Dropping the feed dogs means that you are now in charge of the stitch length and must control it with your hands alone. If you have a speed selector you may find it useful to start a little slower than your usual speed. Begin with some easy overall designs as suggested.

Try drawing your pattern on paper first and then use a practice quilt sandwich before starting on your quilt top. Draw your starting threads to the top so that they will not get tangled in the stitches underneath and can be buried at a later stage. It can be difficult to tell if your presser foot is up or down when using an FMQ foot, so make a special effort to check it is down. At first you may find it difficult to get smooth curves and to keep a regular-size stitch, but this will all come with a little practice and a relaxed attitude.

Free-motion quilting patterns, clockwise from top left: meander, loops, flowers, mussels

finishing

Once you have finished your quilting, trim your excess backing and batting, and square up using your cutter, ruler, and mat.

Binding

This is often the stage that quilters like the least, and sometimes they get this far and then leave the whole thing for months or years, waiting to be bound! I am the opposite: I always want to bind my quilt the minute I finish quilting. I feel as if binding those edges will lock in all the quilty goodness before it leaks out and escapes. It's a very satisfying process and it means you are almost there.

Double-Fold Binding

This is the most common way to bind your quilt. The usual strip width used for this binding is 2½″.

1. Prepare your binding by sewing together strips cut from the width of the fabric until you have enough to go around all 4 sides of your quilt plus approximately 12″. Sew together with diagonal seams. Fold the binding in half, wrong sides together, and press along the whole length.

2. Starting about halfway along one side of your quilt, pin the binding to the right side, aligning the raw edges. Leave an 8″ tail of binding free at the start. Sew a generous ¼″ seam and stop a seam width before the first corner. Reverse a couple of stitches.

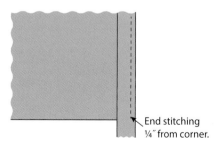

End stitching ¼″ from corner.

3. Pivot the quilt; then fold the binding away from the quilt.

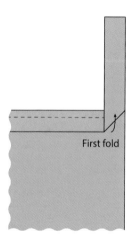

First fold

4. Fold it down on the next edge. This will give you a pleat of fabric at the corner. Begin sewing the next edge from the corner and over the fold. Repeat at each corner.

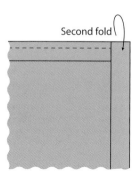

Second fold

5. Stop sewing about 10″ before your starting point, reverse, and cut the thread and binding, leaving another 8″ tail. Bring your 2 tails together and fold back at their meeting place. Finger-press to get a good crease; then carefully hold the tails up and pin them. Sew along the crease, making sure they are still matched up. Trim the tails away, leaving a ¼″ seam, and press open. Finish sewing the binding to the quilt.

6. Fold the binding to the back of the quilt and hold in place using binding clips. Hand sew the binding using a small slip stitch and matching thread, folding the corners over to miter them.

7. If hand sewing the binding is simply too much for you, I suggest you follow this exact process but start from the back of the quilt instead. When all the binding is sewn, fold to the front, clip in place, and topstitch close to the folded edge by machine.

Single-Fold Binding

I like to use a single-fold binding. I find this quicker, easier, and more economical due to using less fabric. I have been using this method for the last 25 years, and the bindings on my quilts are still in good condition!

The process is exactly the same as in the double-fold method but uses strips 1¾″ wide. Since this binding is not as bulky, you can join the strips and the ends with straight seams instead of diagonal seams. The length of binding does not need to be pressed in half. Line up a raw edge with your quilt top and stitch as described in Double-Fold Binding (previous page). When you have finished, turn to the back and fold under the raw edges of the binding. Use binding clips and hand stitch the folded edge to the quilt back. This is a little more fiddly than with the double-fold binding, but it's still quicker than pressing that long strip in half!

Washing and Storing Quilts

There should be no problem putting your quilt into the washing machine and tumble dryer once finished. Use a cold wash and throw in some color catchers for your quilt's first wash, and then tumble dry on a gentle heat. This process will give your quilt a slightly crinkly appearance that is very pleasing.

Try not to store your quilts folded for long periods if possible. They should be on the bed, over the sofa, or in the car, being used and loved. If you do need to store them, rolling is the best option, and if they have to be folded, try doing this with diagonal folds rather than straight ones.

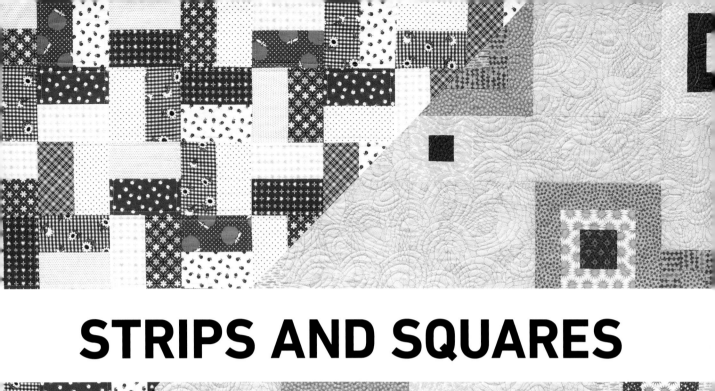

STRIPS AND SQUARES

Semaphore Crib Quilt

Finished block: 10″ × 10″
Finished quilt: 40½″ × 50½″

It's good to start small, and this fat quarter–friendly crib quilt is the perfect first quilt to get you started on your patchwork journey. The simple cross shape is created by stitching rectangles together and then rotating them. When finished, each block looked to me like it was doing semaphore code, hence the name. Red, white, and blue is the perfect gender-neutral color palette—not too babyish, and, along with the generous size, ensures this quilt won't be outgrown for a long time.

MATERIALS

Assorted white prints: 5 fat quarters

Assorted blue prints: 4 fat quarters

Assorted red prints: 4 fat quarters

Binding: ½ yard

Backing: 1⅝ yards

Batting: 44″ × 54″

CUTTING

Assorted white prints

From the shortest (18″) side of the fat quarters:

• Cut a total of 30 strips 3″ × 18″.

Assorted blue prints

From the shortest (18″) side of the fat quarters:

• Cut a total of 15 strips 3″ × 18″.

Assorted red prints

From the shortest (18″) side of the fat quarters:

• Cut a total of 15 strips 3″ × 18″.

Binding

• Cut 5 strips 2½″ × width of fabric.

FABRICS: Sunnyside Ave. collection by Amy Smart for Penny Rose Fabrics

construction

Block Assembly

1. Sew together 1 blue strip and 1 white strip. Press. Repeat to make 15 blue strip sets. Repeat with the red and white strips to make 15 red strip sets.

2. From each strip set, cut 3 squares 5½″ × 5½″.

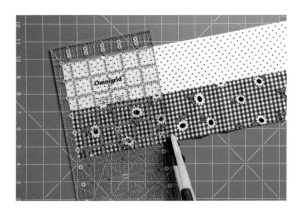

3. Cut 40 blue/white squares and 40 red/white squares.

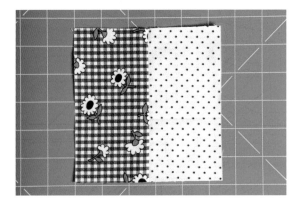

4. Arrange and sew together 4 squares to make each block. Make 10 blue/white blocks and 10 red/white blocks.

Quilt Construction

Arrange and sew the blocks into 5 rows of 4 blocks each, alternating the colors. Press. Join the rows and press.

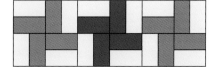

Quilt assembly

Finishing

Layer, quilt, and bind as desired. This quilt was finished by machine using a walking foot to stitch a straight-line grid, with lines a ¼″ on either side of the seamlines.

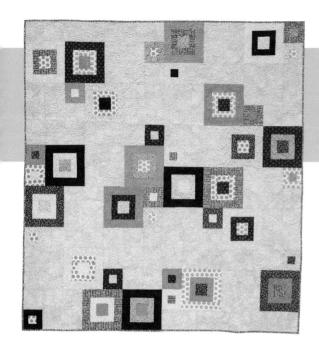

Zen Garden Quilt

Finished blocks: 5″ × 5″ and 10″ × 10″

Finished quilt: 70½″ × 75½″

This über-modern version of a Log Cabin pattern looks really complicated but is actually very straightforward and super speedy to make. There are just two simple block designs, which are sewn together with background blocks to create a larger panel. Though the blocks appear to float at random on the background, the quilt is made of just four of these large panels: one in each quarter, with two rotated. We will make our way through this impressive quilt stage by stage, unlocking the mysteries of construction.

MATERIALS

Assorted bright prints: 20 fat quarters for blocks

Gray print: 2½ yards for background

Binding: ¾ yard

Backing (pieced crosswise): 4½ yards

Batting: 78″ × 83″

CUTTING

Assorted bright prints

From the longest (20″) side of each of the fat quarters:

- Cut 1 strip 3½″ × 20″; subcut into 20 squares 3½″ × 3½″ for the centers of the large blocks.

- Cut 3 strips 2½″ × 20″; subcut into 20 squares 2½″ × 2½″ for the centers of the small blocks and 40 rectangles 2½″ × 6½″ and 40 rectangles 2½″ × 10½″ for the outer pieces on the large blocks*.

- Cut 3 strips 2″ × 20″; subcut into 40 rectangles 2″ × 2½″ and 40 rectangles 2″ × 5½″ for the outer pieces on the small blocks* and 40 rectangles 2″ × 3½″ and 40 rectangles 2″ × 6½″ for the inner pieces on the large blocks*.

Gray print

- Cut 4 strips 10½″ × width of fabric; subcut into 16 squares 10½″ × 10½″.

- Cut 7 strips 5½″ × width of fabric; subcut into 8 squares 5½″ × 5½″, 8 rectangles 5½″ × 15½″, and 2 rectangles 5½″ × 35½″.

Binding

- Cut 8 strips 2½″ × width of fabric.

* Cut 2 of each size of rectangle from matching fabric for each block.

FABRICS: Blocks: Paintbox Basics and Reef collections by Elizabeth Hartman for Robert Kaufman Fabrics; Background: Gleaned Parakeet in Ash by Carolyn Friedlander for Robert Kaufman Fabrics

construction

Block Assembly

1. Sew 2 rectangles 2″ × 2½″ to either side of a center square 2½″ × 2½″. Press.

2. Sew 2 matching 2″ × 5½″ rectangles to the remaining sides of the center square. Make 20 small blocks.

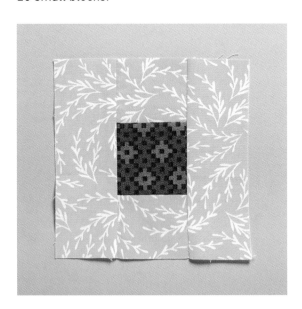

3. Sew 2 rectangles 2″ × 3½″ to either side of a center square 3½″ × 3½″. Press. Sew 2 matching 2″ × 6½″ rectangles to the remaining sides of the center square and press.

4. Using a different fabric, sew 2 rectangles 2½″ × 6½″ to either side of the unit made in Step 3. Press.

5. Sew 2 matching 2½″ × 10½″ rectangles to the remaining sides of the unit. Make 20 large blocks.

Constructing the Quarter Panels

1. Arrange and sew 2 large blocks, 2 small blocks, and 1 gray square 10½″ × 10½″ to make Row 1. Make 4 rows.

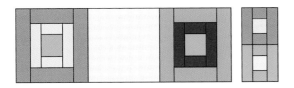

2. Arrange and sew 1 large block, 2 small blocks, 1 gray square 5½″ × 5½″, 2 gray squares 10½″ × 10½″, and 2 gray rectangles 5½″ × 15½″ to make Row 2. Make 4 rows.

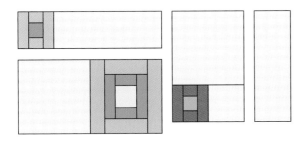

3. Arrange and sew 2 large blocks, 1 small block, 1 gray square 10½″ × 10½″, and 1 gray square 5½″ × 5½″ to make Row 3. Make 4 rows.

 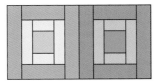

4. Join the rows to make a panel. Make 4.

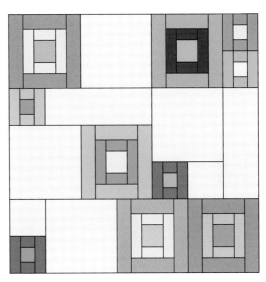

tip ‖ **Beginner Friendly!**

This is a very forgiving quilt with no points to match. It doesn't matter which way up your blocks are and if they end up smaller or larger than your background squares; simply trim your background squares or blocks to fit.

Quilt Construction

1. Turn one panel upside down and sew to the upper edge of another panel. Add a 5½″ × 35½″ gray rectangle to the upper edge to make the left half of the quilt. Press.

2. Turn another panel upside down and sew to the lower edge of the remaining panel. Add a 5½″ × 35½″ gray rectangle the lower edge to make the right half of the quilt. Press.

3. Arrange and sew the halves of the quilt together. Press.

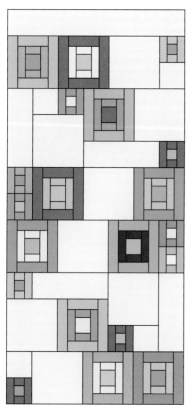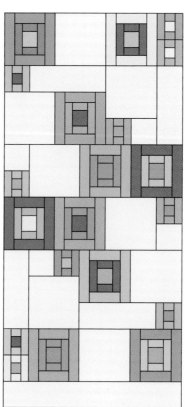

Quilt assembly

Finishing

Layer, quilt, and bind as desired. This quilt was finished by machine using an overall free-motion quilting pattern of interlocking rainbows.

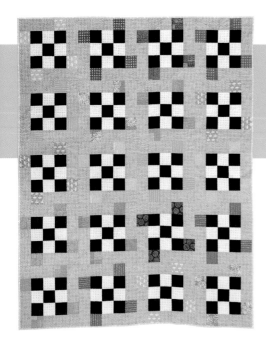

Dancing Pandas Quilt

Finished block: 15″ × 15″

Finished quilt: 60½″ × 75½″

We will be taking our strip-piecing techniques a step further and combining methods learned in both previous projects to make this bright, happy quilt. Black and white strips are sewn together before cutting segments to create checkerboard nine-patch centers. The addition of a colored square to each side gives the illusion that the squares are dancing from foot to foot. Originally, this quilt was called *Dancing Squares*, but when I showed it to my son, Jacob, he renamed it *Dancing Pandas* because of the black-and-white centers! This would make a perfect quilt for a child's single bed.

MATERIALS

White print: 1 yard

Black print: 1¼ yards

Gray print: 2¼ yards

Assorted bright prints: 1 yard total

Binding: ¾ yard

Backing (pieced crosswise): 4 yards

Batting: 68″ × 83″

CUTTING

White print

- Cut 8 strips 3½″ × width of fabric.

Black print

- Cut 10 strips 3½″ × width of fabric.

Gray print

- Cut 21 strips 3½″ × width of fabric; subcut into 60 rectangles 3½″ × 9½″, 20 rectangles 3½″ × 6½″, and 20 squares 3½″ × 3½″.

Assorted bright prints

- Cut 80 squares 3½″ × 3½″ in groups of 4 of the same fabric.

Binding

- Cut 8 strips 2½″ × width of fabric.

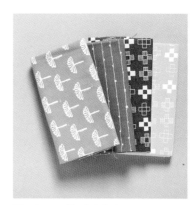

Blueberry Park fabrics

FABRIC: Blueberry
Park collection by
Karen Lewis for
Robert Kaufman
Fabrics

construction

Block Assembly

Make the Nine-Patch Centers

1. Sew 2 black strips to 1 white strip. Press to the black strips. Make 4 strip sets.

2. Sew 2 white strips to 1 black strip. Press to the black strip. Make 2 strips sets.

tip ‖ **Make It Easy**

You may find it easier to cut your black and white strips in half to give you 2 shorter lengths before sewing together into strip sets.

3. Cut the strip sets into 3½″ segments. Cut 40 total from the strip sets made in Step 1 and 20 total from the strip sets made in Step 2.

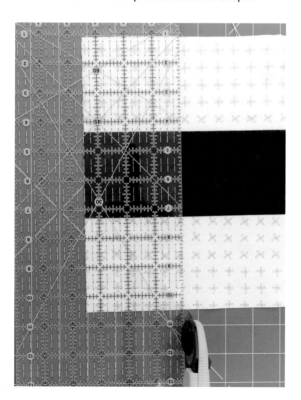

4. Arrange and sew the segments together, nesting the seams. Press the seams outward. Make 20 nine-patch centers.

Finish the Block

1. Sew a bright print square to a 3½″ × 6½″ gray rectangle. Sew to the nine-patch center.

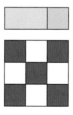

2. Sew a bright print square to one end of a 3½″ × 9½″ gray rectangle. Sew to the nine-patch center.

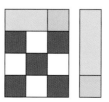

3. Sew a bright print square to one end of another 3½″ × 9½″ gray rectangle. Sew to the nine-patch center.

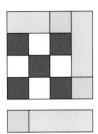

4. Sew a bright print square between a 3½″ × 3½″ gray square and a 3½″ × 9½″ gray rectangle. Sew to the nine-patch center to complete the block. Make 20 blocks.

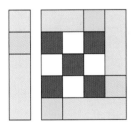

Quilt Construction

Arrange and sew the blocks into 5 rows of 4 blocks each. Press. Join the rows and press.

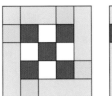
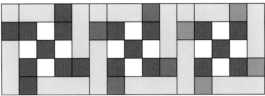

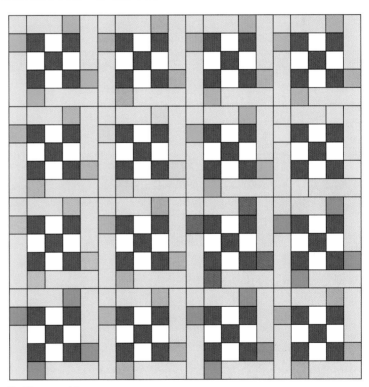

Quilt assembly

Finishing

Layer, quilt, and bind as desired. This quilt was finished by machine using a walking foot to stitch parallel wavy lines along the length of the quilt.

TRIANGLES

Tree of Paradise Quilt

Finished quilt: 67½˝ × 82½˝

Red-and-white quilts have a wonderful way of appearing both very modern and very traditional at the same time. This traditional Tree of Paradise design is often used as a repeating block on a much smaller scale, but I've super-sized and simplified the design to make a really striking quilt that's still quick to make. It's designed as a perfect half-square triangle (HST) starter project, as the units are large and (almost!) the whole design is made up of these (plus simple squares and rectangles). We are using on-point blocks for the first time here but again on a very large scale to help get you started. This would also look fabulous in blue and white or even pink and white! Although the background of this quilt appears white, it is actually Kona Cotton in Snow, which is a very pale cream, to give a traditional feel.

MATERIALS

Red solid: 2 yards

White solid: 5 yards

Binding: ¾ yard

Backing: 5¼ yards

Batting: 75˝ × 90˝

CUTTING

Red solid

- Cut 5 strips 6˝ × width of fabric; subcut into 29 squares 6˝ × 6˝.

- Cut 1 strip 6½˝ × width of fabric; subcut into 1 square 6½˝ × 6½˝. Trim the remaining strip to 5½˝; subcut 4 squares 5½˝ × 5½˝.

- Cut 7 strips 3˝ × width of fabric for the border.

White solid

- Cut 5 strips 6˝ × width of fabric; subcut into 28 squares 6˝ × 6˝.

- Cut 1 strip 6½˝ × width of fabric; subcut into 1 square 6½˝ × 6½˝.

- Cut 5 strips 5½˝ × width of fabric; subcut into 12 squares 5½˝ × 5½˝, 2 rectangles 5½˝ × 10½˝, 2 rectangles 5½˝ × 15½˝, and 2 rectangles 5½˝ × 20½˝. (For best use of fabric, cut the longest pieces first.)

- Cut 1 strip 10½˝ × width of fabric; subcut into 2 squares 10½˝ × 10½˝.

- Cut 2 strips 30˝ × width of fabric; subcut into 2 squares 30˝ × 30˝ and cut each in half diagonally to make 4 triangles.

- Cut 8 strips 3½˝ × width of fabric for the border.

Binding

- Cut 8 strips 2½˝ × width of fabric.

FABRICS: Kona
Cotton solids from
Robert Kaufman
Fabrics

2-IN-1 HST

1. Add 1″ to the desired finished size of the triangle units. Cut a square this size for each of 2 fabrics. Place right sides together with the lighter-colored square on top. Mark a diagonal line from corner to corner on the wrong side of the top square.

2. Stitch a ¼″ seam on either side of this line.

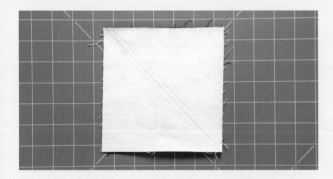

3. Cut on the marked line, open, and press. This will make 2 HST units.

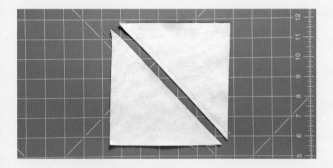

4. Trim both units to the required size (the finished size plus seam allowances).

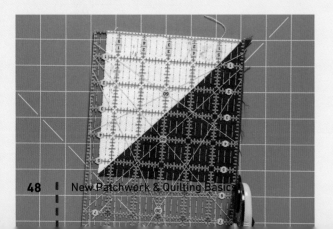

construction

Block Assembly

1. Using the 2-in-1 HST method, 28 red squares 6″ × 6″, and 28 white squares 6″ × 6″, make 56 HST units. Trim each to a square 5½″ × 5½″.

2. Make 2 HST units using a red square 6½″ × 6½″ and a white square 6½″ × 6½″; discard one of the units. Trim the HST unit to 6″ × 6″ and layer with the remaining 6″ × 6″ red square. Mark a diagonal line on the wrong side of the top square. Stitch a ¼″ seam on both sides of the line.

3. Cut on the marked line. Open and press.

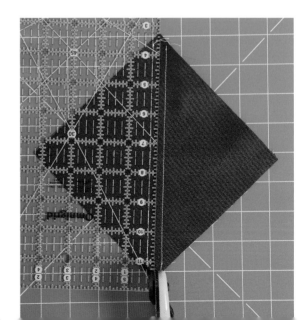

4. Trim to 5½″ × 5½″. Make 2 quarter-square triangle (QST) variation units.

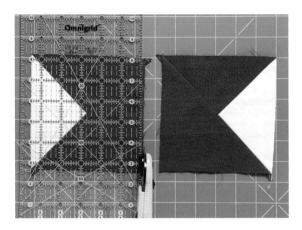

5. Arrange and sew together 20 HST units from Step 1 and 5 white squares 5½″ × 5½″ to make the top unit. Make 1. Press.

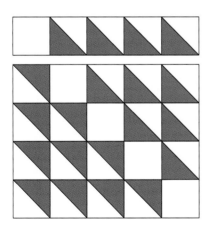

6. Arrange and sew together 15 HST units from Step 1, 1 white square 5½″ × 5½″, 1 white rectangle 5½″ × 10½″, 1 white rectangle 5½″ × 15½″, and 1 white rectangle 5½″ × 20½″ to make the side unit. Make 2.

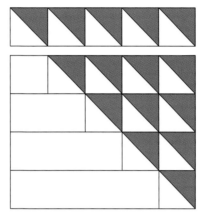

7. Arrange and sew together 6 HST units from Step 1, 2 QST variation units from Steps 2–4, 4 red squares 5½″ × 5½″, 5 white squares 5½″ × 5½″, and 2 white squares 10½″ × 10½″ to make the bottom unit. Make 1.

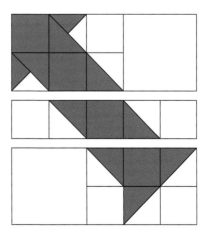

Quilt Construction

1. Arrange and sew together the units. Press. Sew the large white triangles to the edges, starting at the top and bottom corners. Trim the excess white rectangles on the sides and any excess white triangle fabric to measure 56½″ × 71½″ for the quilt center.

Tip || **Stitching Bias-Cut Edges**

Be especially careful sewing the triangles, as these are bias edges that will naturally stretch. Use plenty of pins and go slowly.

2. Sew together the red strips 3″ × width of fabric to make one long length. Cut 2 strips 3″ × 56½″ for the top and bottom borders and 2 strips 3″ × 76½″ for the side borders.

3. Sew the red top and bottom borders to the quilt top. Press. Sew the red side borders to the quilt top. Press.

4. Sew together the white strips 3½″ × width of fabric to make one long length. Cut 2 strips 3½″ × 61½″ for the top and bottom borders and 2 strips 3½″ × 82½″ for the side borders.

5. Sew the white top and bottom borders to the quilt top. Press. Sew the white side borders to the quilt top. Press.

Quilt assembly

Finishing

Layer, quilt, and bind as desired. This quilt was hand quilted with a 2″ diagonal grid pattern using Aurifil 12-weight thread in a cream shade.

Pop Art Block Keeper

Finished block: 9″ × 9″
Finished block keeper: 18″ × 38″

Now that you know how to make patchwork blocks, it's time to make some storage for them. This roomy block keeper will keep your blocks organized and in good condition while you continue working on your quilt. It can also be taken along to classes and is especially useful for long-running sampler-quilt projects. A great way to try out more half-square triangle techniques, this project uses the 8-in-1 technique, which is extra speedy. The vibrant, colorful blocks are inspired by the type of pop art pictures created by Andy Warhol. Though only two different HST units are used throughout (orange/turquoise and yellow/pink), the piece still appears complex and fascinating due to the endless possibilities of the HST unit.

MATERIALS

Turquoise, orange, pink, and yellow solids: ⅓ yard each

Blue, red, and dark pink solids: ⅛ yard each

Green solid: ¼ yard

Flannel: 2 yards

Fusible interfacing: ¼ yard

Bosal foam stabilizer: ½ yard

Black oval elastic (³⁄₁₆″): ½ yard

Black round elastic (⅛″): 1 yard

Wooden toggle buttons: 3

Batting: 20″ × 40″

Fabric and toggle buttons

CUTTING

Turquoise, orange, pink, and yellow solids

- Cut 3 squares 8″ × 8″ from each color for the blocks.

- Cut 4 squares 3½″ × 3½″ from each color for the blocks.

Blue, red, and dark pink solids

- Cut 2 squares 3½″ × 3½″ from each color for the blocks.

Green solid

- Cut 2 squares 3½″ × 3½″ for the blocks.

- Cut 1 rectangle 2½″ × 18½″ for the spine.

- Cut 2 rectangles 3½″ × 14½″ for the handles.

Flannel

- Cut 1 piece 18½″ × 38½″.

- Cut 3 pieces 16″ × 34″ using pinking shears or a pinking rotary blade.

Fusible interfacing

- Cut 2 pieces 3″ × 14″.

Bosal foam stabilizer

- Cut 1 piece 18″ × 38″.

tip || Body Building

Bosal fusible foam stabilizer is used as an interfacing to give body, form, and structure to items such as bags.

FABRICS: Kona Cotton solids from Robert Kaufman Fabrics

8-IN-1 HST

1. Add 1″ to the desired finished size of the triangle units. Double the measurement and cut a square this size from each of 2 fabrics. Place right sides together with the lighter-colored square on top. Mark a diagonal line from corner to corner on the wrong side of the top square. Mark a second diagonal line from the other 2 corners to cross the center of the square. Stitch a ¼″ seam on either side of both lines.

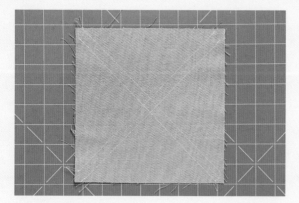

2. Make a vertical cut through the center of the square to cut it in half.

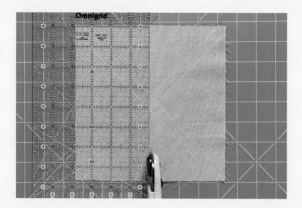

3. Without disturbing the halves, pivot the ruler and make a horizontal cut through the center of the square to cut it in quarters.

4. Cut on the diagonal lines to make 8 units.

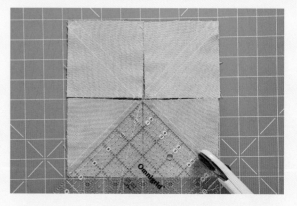

5. Open, press, and trim to the required size.

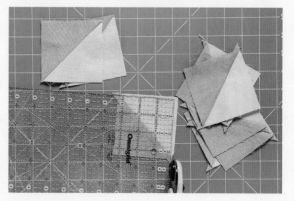

construction

Block Assembly

1. Using the 8-in-1 HST method and the pink and yellow squares 8″ × 8″, make 24 HST units. Make 24 HST units using the turquoise and orange squares 8″ × 8″. Open and press; then trim the HST units to 3½″ × 3½″.

2. Arrange and sew together 6 pink/yellow HST units, 2 yellow squares 3½″ × 3½″, and 1 dark pink square 3½″ × 3½″. Press. Make 2 blocks.

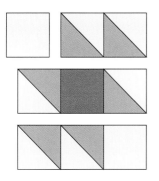

3. Arrange and sew together 6 pink/yellow HST units, 2 pink squares 3½″ × 3½″, and 1 green square 3½″ × 3½″. Press. Make 2 blocks.

4. Arrange and sew together 6 turquoise/ orange HST units, 2 orange squares 3½″ × 3½″, and 1 blue square 3½″ × 3½″. Press. Make 2 blocks.

5. Arrange and sew together 6 turquoise/ orange HST units, 2 turquoise squares 3½″ × 3½″, and 1 red square 3½″ × 3½″. Press. Make 2 blocks.

6. Arrange and sew together the blocks in 2 rows of 2 blocks each. Press. Join the rows and press. Make 2 large blocks.

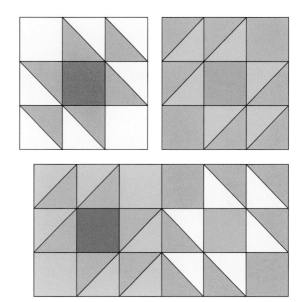

Block Keeper Assembly

1. Sew the green rectangle 2½″ × 18½″ between the 2 large blocks. Place on top of the batting and spray or pin baste to secure. Mark a diagonal grid for quilting using a ruler and Hera Marker or water-soluble pen; use the block seamlines as a guide. Machine quilt along the marked lines. There is no need to use a backing fabric, but if your sewing machine prefers one, then feel free to use a thin muslin or calico. Trim the excess batting even with the top.

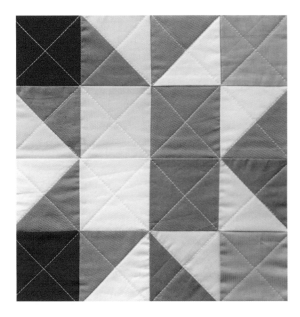

2. Place a fusible interfacing piece on the wrong side of each green rectangle 3½″ × 14½″, making sure ¼″ of green shows on each long edge. Flip the pieces and press from the fabric side until the interfacing adheres. Turn the piece over and press ¼″ of the green fabric over the interfacing on both edges. Use just the tip of your iron to avoid melting the interfacing (you may want to turn your iron down).

3. Fold the green rectangle in half lengthwise, wrong sides together, so that the folded edges meet. Pin and topstitch close to the folded edges. Topstitch the other edge to match. Make 2 handles.

4. Pin the ends of the handle pieces to the short edges of the quilted top, raw edges even. Place them on the seams of the second and third squares in from each long edge. Stitch in place using an ⅛″ seam.

5. Cut the thicker elastic into 3 pieces 4″ long. Fold in half and pin to the quilted top in the center of the top, bottom, and side edges of one of the large pieced blocks. Stitch in place using an ⅛″ seam.

6. Following the manufacturer's instructions, center and fuse the foam stabilizer to the batting side of the quilted top. If the adhesive won't stick very well, use some basting spray to hold in place.

7. Place the flannel piece 18½″ × 38½″ right sides together with the quilted top. Pin the edges, making sure the handles and elastic loops are tucked well away from the edge. Sew using a ¼″ seam, leaving a 9″ opening on one of the long edges. Trim the seam allowance at the corners at an angle. Carefully turn right side out, trying not to disturb the foam stabilizer too much.

8. Pin the opening closed and topstitch close to the edge around the whole piece.

9. Mark a line in the center of the green spine piece. Mark a line on either side to make 3 equally spaced lines. Center one of the pinked-edge flannel pieces on the flannel side of the quilted top. Pin in place. Turn to the right side and stitch on the center marked line on the spine to attach it. Turn to the flannel side and fold the flannel leaf to the left and pin another flannel piece in place. Turn to the right side and stitch on a marked line on the spine to attach it. Repeat with the remaining flannel piece.

10. Sew the 3 toggle buttons in place on the other half of the block keeper opposite the elastic loops. Sew one end of the thin elastic around one of the toggle buttons on a long side. Stretch the other end of the elastic across the inside of the block keeper and tie a loop in the other end so that it can be secured over the toggle button opposite it; trim the ends of the elastic. The elastic will help hold your blocks in place. Use the flannel leaves to organize your blocks. You can add more of these at any stage if you wish.

Pinhole Stars Quilt

Finished block: 12″ × 12″

Finished quilt: 72½″ × 72½″

The star is one of the most enduring patchwork motifs and offers endless variations. Here it gains a modern twist with an off-center square in the middle. Setting the jewellike stars in a dark background gives the impression that you are staring at the night sky. Extending the space around each block with the same dark background accentuates this effect and gives us a chance to try sashing for the first time. This block gives you plenty of opportunity to practice making Flying Geese units using the 4-in-1 method, and you can continue using your patchwork skills for the center units. Have fun collecting the bright prints for the sparkling stars; I used eleven different prints, making two blocks each of eight of them and three blocks each with my three favorites!

MATERIALS

Dark print: 4¼ yards for background, sashing, and borders

Assorted bright prints: 2½ yards total for blocks

Binding: ¾ yard

Backing: 4½ yards

Batting: 80″ × 80″

CUTTING

Dark print

- Cut 5 strips 7½″ × width of fabric; subcut into 25 squares 7½″ × 7½″.

- Cut 10 strips 3½″ × width of fabric; subcut into 100 squares 3½″ × 3½″.

- Cut 2 strips 2½″ × width of fabric; subcut into 25 squares 2½″ × 2½″.

- Cut 7 strips 2½″ × width of fabric; subcut into 20 strips 2½″ × 12½″ for the sashing.

- Cut 15 strips 2½″ × width of fabric for the sashing and borders.

Assorted bright prints (per block—25 blocks total)

- Cut 1 rectangle 1½″ × 2½″.

- Cut 1 rectangle 1½″ × 3½″.

- Cut 1 square 3½″ × 3½″.

- Cut 1 rectangle 3½″ × 6½″.

- Cut 4 squares 4″ × 4″.

Binding

- Cut 8 strips 2½″ × width of fabric.

FABRICS: Judith's Fancy collection by Jennifer Paganelli for FreeSpirit Fabrics

4-IN-1 FLYING GEESE UNITS

1. Mark a diagonal line from corner to corner on the back of each of 4 bright print squares 4″ × 4″. Place 2 squares 4″ × 4″ right sides together with a dark print square 7½″ × 7½″. Sew a ¼″ seam on either side of the marked line.

2. Cut on the marked line to make 2 halves. Press the seams toward the bright print triangles.

3. Place another square 4″ × 4″ right sides together with the one of the units from Step 2. Sew a ¼″ seam on either side of the marked line.

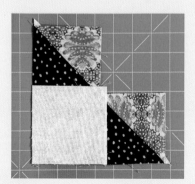

4. Cut on the marked line, open, and press to complete 2 Flying Geese units.

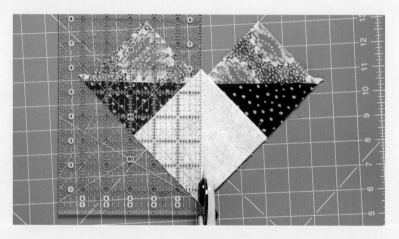

Repeat Steps 3 and 4 with the other half and the remaining square 4″ × 4″ to make 2 more Flying Geese units.

5. Trim each unit to an accurate 3½″ × 6½″.

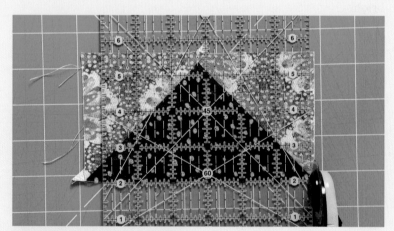

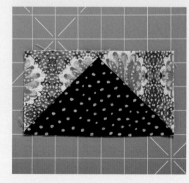

note Follow this simple formula for making Flying Geese units in different sizes: Add 1″ to the finished size of the square for the small triangles and 1½″ to the finished size of the square for the large triangle. Sew and cut as shown. Trim the sewn units to the required size (finished size plus seam allowance).

construction

Block Assembly

1. Sew a bright print rectangle 1½″ × 2½″ to a dark print square 2½″ × 2½″. Press.

2. Working in a clockwise direction, sew a bright print rectangle 1½″ × 3½″ to the block center. Press.

3. Sew a bright print square 3½″ × 3½″ to the block center. Press.

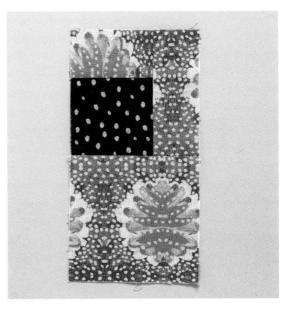

4. Sew a bright print rectangle 3½″ × 6½″ to complete the block. Press.

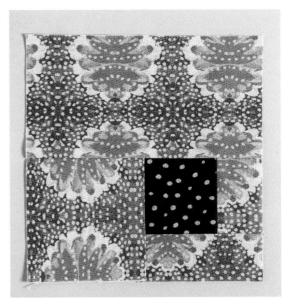

5. Arrange and sew 2 Flying Geese units to the block center. Press toward the center.

6. Arrange and sew 4 dark print squares 3½″ × 3½″ to the ends of 2 Flying Geese units. Press toward the squares.

7. Join the rows to complete the block. Press toward the block center. Make 25 blocks.

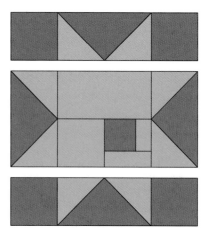

Quilt Construction

1. Arrange the blocks into 5 rows of 5 blocks each, making sure the center dark-print square is in the same place in each. Sew a dark-print sashing strip 2½″ × 12½″ between the blocks in each row. Press toward the sashing.

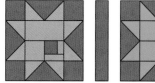 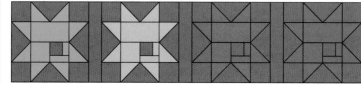

2. Sew together the dark print strips 2½″ × width of fabric to make one long length. Cut 6 strips 2½″ × 68½″ for the sashing and the top and bottom borders and 2 strips 2½″ × 72½″ for the side borders.

3. Pin and sew the sashing pieces between the rows. Pin and sew the top and bottom borders to the quilt center. Press. Pin and sew the side borders to the quilt center. Press.

Quilt assembly

Finishing

Layer, quilt, and bind as desired. This quilt was finished by machine using an overall free-motion quilting pattern of kissing stars.

SKILL BUILDING

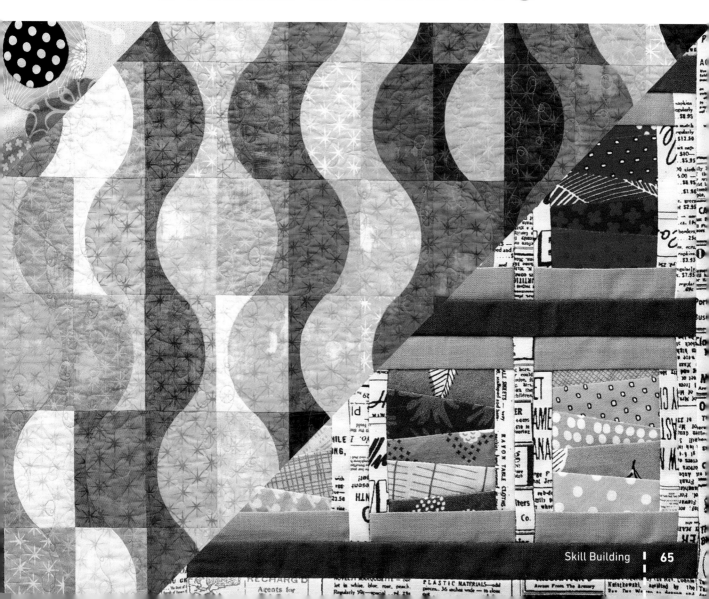

Appliqué

Appliqué comes from the French word "to apply" and describes stitching a small piece of fabric to a larger one. As any shape can be used, it allows for more creative designs, far from the rigid geometry of patchwork. It is one of my favorite quilting techniques, especially when worked by hand. I am a big fan of "slow stitching" and like nothing better than some quiet sofa time with my latest appliqué project.

turned-edge appliqué

Also called *needle-turn appliqué*, this is a traditional hand-sewing technique in which the raw edges of the fabric piece are turned under and stitched to the background fabric at the same time. There are many ways to help with this task and to prepare shapes by turning edges under prior to sewing. The simplest way is to pinch under the edge an inch or so ahead of your stitching to give you a fold where your seamline would be. For many awkward shapes, this is the best and quickest way, but simple shapes can benefit from these techniques.

Paper Method

Circles are one of the hardest shapes to appliqué well. This method helps you achieve perfect curves, especially with tiny circles.

1. Make a paper template using the inner line on the pattern. Cut the fabric circle using the outer line on the pattern. With the wrong side of the fabric circle toward you and using a double thread, knot securely; then sew small running stitches ⅛″ away from the edge.

2. Place the paper template in the center and gently gather the stitches and secure your thread. Press from both sides. Carefully pop out the paper piece and your circle is ready to stitch!

Card-and-Foil Method

The following method is better for large circles but can also be used for other curved shapes, such as leaves.

1. Make a template from thin card stock using the inner line on the pattern. Cut the fabric piece using the outer line on the pattern. Place your fabric piece wrong side up on a piece of aluminum foil. Place your template on top of the fabric piece and carefully enclose it in the foil, pressing tightly all the way round.

2. Press both sides of this foil packet very well, using the highest setting on your iron.

Carefully unwrap the foil (it will be hot!) and take out the fabric piece. If needed, you can gently give the folded edges another press. Using spray starch or Flatter spray prior to pressing will also help.

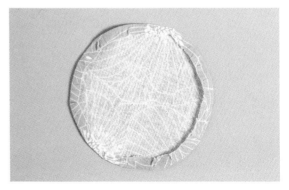

Hand Stitching Your Appliqué Pieces

The aim is to make your stitches as invisible as possible, and you will find that a fine needle and a fine thread that matches the appliqué piece will be a huge help with this (see Toolbox, page 10). Pin the pieces in place and turn under a scant ¼″ of the edge. Moving from right to left (if you are right-handed), make a tiny straight stitch close to the folded edge that just catches the edge of fabric and fixes it to the background below. The travelling stitches happen on the back of the background fabric and should be between ⅛″ and ¼″ in length. Keep the stitches on the front neat and straight (*no slanting!*) and give a little tug to make sure they are secure, as loose stitches will show more.

I use the outer line on the patterns to cut my pieces and simply eyeball the amount to turn under. If the placement of the appliqué pieces needs to be exact, trace the design on the background fabric using an erasable marker. As you turn under the appliqué pieces, match the fold to the marks.

Dealing with Points and V Shapes

Difficulties with turned-edge appliqué occur at points, such as the tips of leaves, and at the V shapes between the petals of flowers. The first difficulty is caused by too much fabric under the seam and the second by not having enough.

Points

1. Stop stitching at least ½″ before you reach the point. Fold the fabric seam on the other side of the point under before folding the fabric seam on the side you are working on; this will give you a dog-ear at the tip on the other side of the point. Continue stitching to the point, holding this in place.

2. As you turn at the point to begin stitching on the other edge, use your needle to fold or roll the dog-ear under the seam until it is hidden completely. Continue stitching the other edge.

V Shapes

Stop stitching at least ½″ before you reach the V on the shape and use small embroidery scissors to snip the seam allowance—almost the whole width of it. Use your needle to "swoop" under the seam allowance at the point of the V; this will fold under all the raw edges of the fabric so that you can stitch even the tiniest seam. Stitch and swoop until you are at the V, and use one tiny stitch to fix it there. You will also need to snip your seam allowance when stitching concave curves.

Tip || **Wet and Wonderful**

I find wetting my needle helps when turning my fabric under, especially at a V shape. But don't put needles in your mouth; instead have a small damp sponge near to you while sewing.

raw-edge appliqué with fusible web

Hand stitching isn't for everyone, and you can make perfectly lovely appliqué using your machine and not turning your edges under. The best way is to use a paper-backed fusible web to hold your pieces in place before finishing the edges with a range of stitches.

1. Using the inner lines on the pattern, trace the shapes on the paper side of the fusible web.

2. Press the marked fusible web, paper side up, on the wrong side of your fabric.

3. Carefully cut out the shape using small sharp scissors and peel away the paper. Place in position on the background fabric. Press to fuse the shapes to the background.

4. Stitch around the edges of the shapes using a top stitch, blanket stitch, zigzag, or blind hem stitch.

Flower Garland Pillow

Finished pillow: 18″ × 18″

I first became aware of antique quilts through the collection at the American Museum & Gardens in Bath, England. They have a wonderful collection, and I especially fell in love with their beautiful versions of Baltimore Album Quilts. These traditionally feature appliqué blocks of flowers and leaves, often arranged in garland or ring shapes. Since then, I have designed many of my own modern versions of this block, and they never fail to please either in the finished look of the piece or the enjoyment I've gained from making them. This is my simplest version yet, designed to give you a confident start to what I hope will be a lifetime of appliqué appreciation. The three simple shapes (leaf, circle, and flower) should give you experience enough for all your future stitching. I chose a cotton/flax fabric for my background for the texture.

MATERIALS

Cotton/flax print: 1 yard for background and backing

Green print: 1 fat quarter for leaves

Assorted coral prints: ⅛ yard total for flowers

Yellow prints: ⅛ yard total for flowers

Orange prints: ⅛ yard total for flowers

Black-and-white prints: ⅛ yard total for flower centers

Charcoal prints: ⅛ yard total for flower centers

Water-erasable pen

18″ pillow form

Patterns A–F (pages 122 and 123)

Placement pattern (page 122)

CUTTING

Cotton/flax print

- Cut 1 square 20″ × 20″ for the pillow-front background.
- Cut 2 rectangles 13″ × 19″ for the pillow back.

Green print

- Cut 12 leaves using pattern A.

Assorted coral prints

- Cut 4 circle flowers using pattern B.

Yellow prints

- Cut 8 circle flowers using pattern C.

Orange prints

- Cut 4 flowers using pattern E.

Black-and-white prints

- Cut 8 flower centers using pattern D.

Charcoal prints

- Cut 4 flower centers using pattern F.

FABRICS: Background:
Sevenberry Canvas
Cotton/Flax Prints
by Sevenberry from
Robert Kaufman Fabrics

construction

Pillow Front Assembly

1. Fold the background square 20″ × 20″ in quarters and crease the folds. Trace the placement pattern onto your fabric square one-quarter at a time, using the folded lines as a guide. A lightbox is a great help with this. If you don't have one, try taping to either a window or your computer screen with the brightness turned up. It also helps to go over the pattern lines with a thicker pen. The pattern is just a guide and does not need to be too accurate.

2. Prepare the 12 green leaves using pattern A. See the tips for stitching points (page 68). There is no need to stitch the areas that will be covered by subsequent layers of flowers. Trim away the excess leaf fabric.

3. Using the paper method (page 66), prepare the 4 coral circle flowers and stitch in place.

tip || **Light It Up!**

Make a quick and easy lightbox to help with your tracing. Take a small, shallow cardboard box without a lid and pop your phone inside it with the flashlight function switched on. Place a piece of glass or clear acrylic (a large square patchwork ruler works well) on the box and trace your pattern on top of this!

----

4. Using the card-and-foil method (page 67), prepare the 8 yellow circle flowers and stitch in place.

5. Using the paper method, prepare the 8 black-and-white flower centers and stitch in place.

6. Stitch the 4 orange flowers in place. See the tips for V shapes (page 69).

7. Using the paper method, prepare the 4 charcoal flower centers and stitch in place.

8. Press the completed pillow front facedown. Trim to a square 19″ × 19″.

Finishing the Pillow

1. On one long edge of both pillow back pieces, turn under ½″ and press. Turn under another ½″ and press. Stitch to make a hem on both pieces.

2. Place the pillow front right side up. Layer the 2 back pieces right side down, with the hemmed edges overlapping in the center.

3. Pin and sew the edges together using a ½″ seam. Trim the excess seam allowance at the corners. Turn right side out and press the edges. Insert the pillow form.

Curved Piecing

Curves have a reputation for being tricky to sew and a little bit scary, but, like most techniques, they just require practice. The addition of curves to a quilt design creates movement and interest and opens up a world of fascinating blocks for you to play with, such as New York Beauty and Double Wedding Ring. The *Stream Quilt* includes a very easy and gentle curved block to get you started. It's a simple one-block pattern, so you will get plenty of curve practice! I've included a troubleshooting section, so if you find the curves aren't coming naturally, try my tips to help you. I would advise you start piecing your curves with plenty of pins and once you get the hang of it, try my one-pin method.

It helps to cut the pieces so that the curves are on the bias of the fabric. The patterns with tighter curves have grainline arrows for placing the pieces.

many-pin method

1. Fold a convex fabric piece in half, *wrong* sides together, and finger-press to mark the center. Repeat with a concave piece but fold in half *right* sides together.

2. Place the concave piece on top of the convex piece, right sides together, lining up the center folds (they should nestle nicely together). Pin.

Place a pin at either end of the seam, lining up the straight edges.

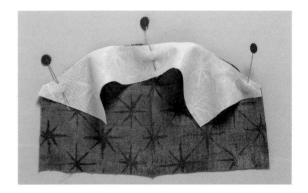

3. Gently smooth out the raw edges between these 3 pinned points, bringing together and lining up both pieces of fabric. Use more pins to secure.

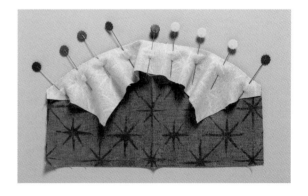

4. Begin sewing with the concave piece on top, gently easing around the curve and making sure you keep the raw edges together. Be care-

ful not to sew any pleats or puckers into the seam and not to stretch the fabric too much.

5. Press toward the concave piece.

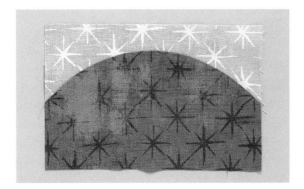

one-pin method

1. Fold and finger-press the pieces in half and pin in the center, as with the previous method.

2. Bring the straight edges together at the start of the seam and hold them in place until anchored by your machine presser foot.

3. Begin to sew slowly and carefully, smoothing and easing the fabric. Once you reach the center pin, remove it and bring together the straight edges at the end of the seam. Pin.

4. Continue smoothing and easing the pieces as you sew to the end pin to complete the curved seam. I find this method gives great accuracy without all the fiddly pinning before sewing each seam.

troubleshooting

The most common issue with curved piecing is making the 2 pieces fit together perfectly. If they don't, this may distort the finished size of the block. Problems are caused by either not keeping the raw edges perfectly lined up as you sew the seam or not managing a consistent ¼″ seam. Both these things will come with practice. Careful pinning, though laborious, should certainly help to begin with.

If you are really struggling, try stitching from the center out to the block edge. Turn the piece over and again sew from the center to the edge. You could also add to the outside edges of the block when cutting and then trim it to the correct size once the block is sewn.

Stream Quilt

Finished block: 5″ × 8″
Finished quilt: 60½″ × 72½″

By using this restricted blue, green, and neutral palette of blender fabrics, I have tried to create the illusion of ripples on a stream, with reflections from trees above and perhaps the odd floating autumn leaf. Feel free to play around with this design; you don't need to keep the exact same layout of rows. Try making your blocks curve in different directions from mine. It would also be easy to increase the size of this quilt by adding extra blocks and rows. This pattern could look equally effective as a bright rainbow scrappy quilt. I would *always* advise making a few test blocks before cutting for the whole quilt.

MATERIALS

Blue, green, turquoise, and neutral prints: ½ yard each of 16 prints

Binding: ⅝ yard

Backing (pieced crosswise): 4 yards

Batting: 68″ × 80″

Patterns A and B (pages 110 and 111)

CUTTING

Blue, green, turquoise, and neutral prints

- Cut 2 strips 8½″ × width of fabric from each print; subcut a total of 108 concave pieces using pattern A and a total of 108 convex pieces using pattern B.

Binding

- Cut 7 strips 2½″ × width of fabric.

construction

Block Assembly

1. Arrange the pieces before sewing. Try to make some of the blocks low contrast by pairing similar (but not the same) fabrics and make some of the blocks high contrast by pairing light and dark fabrics or differing colors of fabric.

2. Using either of the curved-piecing methods (page 74), sew an A piece to a B piece. Make 108 blocks. Check that the blocks are all 5½″ × 8½″, and if not, trim to size.

FABRICS: Grunge
Seeing Stars
collection by
BasicGrey for Moda
Fabrics + Supplies

Quilt Construction

1. Arrange and sew together the blocks to make 12 columns of 9 blocks each. Press. Spend some time arranging your columns to create ripples and movement through the quilt.

2. Join the columns. Press.

Quilt assembly

Finishing

Layer, quilt, and bind as desired. This quilt was finished by machine using free-motion quilting and a pattern of bubbles and loops on parallel wavy lines along the length of the quilt.

Foundation Paper Piecing

Using a foundation for patchwork is not a new technique, although in the past the foundation would have been fabric (or similar) and it would have stayed in place. These days, we tend to use paper, which is a temporary foundation and is removed once the block is finished. The advent of home printers has made this method of piecing very popular.

A FPP pattern is printed on one side of the paper and stitched from this side along the marked lines (which are, of course, easier to see from the front than the back of the paper). The fabric is placed on the reverse of the paper with the right side facing out. If you can understand the logic of this placement, it will help you to remember how to begin FPP. Starting seems to be the hardest bit and where my students often come unstuck!

The pattern consists of numbered sections that must be covered by fabric. This is achieved by sewing on the lines between the sections with the fabric underneath the paper before flipping the fabric over to cover a section. Seams need to be allowed for at this point before the fabric is *trimmed* and the next piece added. The trimming is crucial and the part of the process that beginners can easily forget.

This method of piecing can be confusing to begin with because it seems that you are working upside down and backwards, but persevere! The results achieved will be worth-while, making ridiculously intricate patterns possible and increasing your accuracy.

For the patterns in this book, print the pattern on regular or special foundation piecing paper, such as Carol Doak's Foundation Paper (by C&T Publishing). Trim each pattern on the outer lines. Align and tape together any partial patterns.

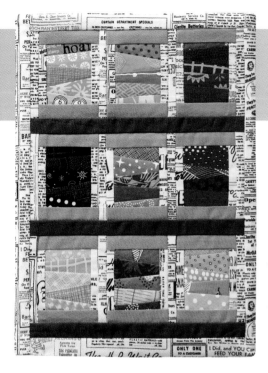

Spool Notebook Holder

Finished size: 11¾″ × 17½″

Foundation paper piecing can be such a fun and versatile method of piecing, but it is also somewhat laborious. Making a small project is a good way to try out the technique without too much pressure. This notebook holder is quick to make once you have pieced your scrappy rainbow Spool blocks. If you are struggling with FPP, you can always make the whole thread section with just one piece of fabric to speed things up. This is a great way to use up some of the scraps you will have accumulated by now, and I hope you will use the finished book to record your future quilt plans.

MATERIALS

Text print: 1 fat quarter

Assorted bright prints: 5 scraps each in 9 colors

Brown solid: ⅛ yard

Charcoal solid: ⅛ yard

Pocket fabric: 1 fat quarter

Lining: 1 fat quarter

Patterns A, B, and C (page 109)

CUTTING

Text print

- Cut 1 rectangle 1″ × 11″.
- Cut 2 rectangles 1⅛″ × 8½″.
- Cut 1 rectangle 10″ × 12¼″.
- Cut the remainder into 3½″ strips to use for the FPP blocks.

Assorted bright prints

- Cut 1 rectangle 1½″ × 2¼″ from each (45 total).

Brown solid

- Cut 1 strip 3″ × 12″ to use for the FPP blocks.

Charcoal solid

- Cut 3 rectangles 1″ × 8½″.

Pocket fabric

- Cut 2 pieces 9″ × 12¼″.

Lining

- Cut 1 piece 12¼″ × 18″.

tip ‖ Size Options

If you want to use a different-size notebook, cut the outer, lining, and pocket pieces up to ¾″ bigger than your notebook size, remembering to include the spine when measuring.

construction

Block Assembly

Print 3 copies each of FPP patterns A, B, and C.

1. Decrease your machine stitch length to 1.5. Starting with foundation A, place a bright print rectangle wrong side down on the unprinted side of the paper pattern. Make sure it covers all of section A1 and overlaps section A2 by at least ¼″.

2. Place and pin a second bright print rectangle of the same color family right sides together with the first rectangle so that, when flipped over at the seamline, the fabric will cover section A2 and overlap section A3 by at least ¼″.

3. Turn the paper pattern over so the printed side is on top. Sew on the line between A1 and A2.

4. Fold and press the fabric so it covers section A2.

5. Fold the paper back at the seamline between sections A2 and A3 and trim the fabric to ¼″ beyond the paper fold.

6. Repeat with another bright print rectangle of the same color family for section A3.

7. Repeat with bright print pieces of the same color family for sections A4 and A5.

8. Continue FPP, using the text print for sections A6 and A7, the brown solid for sections A8 and A9, and the text print for sections A10 and A11. Press.

9. From the paper side of the foundation, trim the excess fabric on the outer line of the pattern.

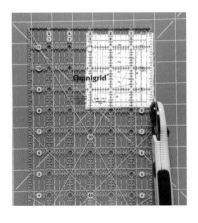

10. Make 3 of pattern A, 3 of pattern B, and 3 of pattern C. Note that the C pieces do not have sections 10 and 11 of the text print.

11. With the papers still in place, arrange and sew together 3 rows of A, B, and C blocks, with C in the middle. Use a pin to match up your pattern lines and sew on the outer line. Remove the papers and press.

12. Sew the charcoal rectangles to the bottom of each row. Join the rows. Press.

Make the Notebook Holder

1. Sew the text print rectangle 1″ × 11″ to the right edge of the block. Sew 2 text print rectangles 1⅛″ × 8½″ to the top and bottom. Sew the text print rectangle 10″ × 12¼″ to the left edge of the block for the back of the notebook holder. Press.

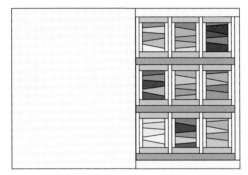

2. Fold and press the pocket rectangles in half on the 9″ side to make 2 pockets 4½″ × 12¼″.

3. Place the lining piece right side up. Position the pocket pieces on the ends, with the folds toward the center. Layer the Spool block piece on top with the right side down.

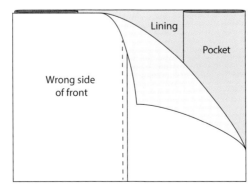

Lining

Pocket

Wrong side of front

4. Pin and sew the layers together, leaving a 6″ opening at the bottom back edge.

5. Trim the seam allowance at the corners to reduce bulk. Turn right side out and press. Check that the cover fits your book well, and make any needed adjustments. Turn under the seam allowances at the opening and hand stitch closed.

MIX AND MATCH

We now have a whole host of quilting skills at our fingertips! Why not mix some of them up to make three stunning intermediate quilts? We'll start by combining simple strips and appliqué in the minimalist *Autumn Trees* quilt. Next up is a spot of FPP and curves as we reinterpret two intricate traditional block designs to create the maximalist *Pinball Wizard* quilt. Lastly, we'll combine a little bit of everything we've learned so far and complete our showstopping row quilt, *Bedding Plants*.

Autumn Trees Quilt

Finished quilt: 55½" × 70½"

A decade ago we moved to a 7-acre plot in the Scottish countryside. Instead of farming animals or planting vegetables, we chose to plant 3,500 trees, mainly because we just love trees! Over the last few years, I have watched them grow into beautiful pockets of woodland that I can now hide inside. My favorite is our birches and their pale stripy trunks that inspired this quilt. Their leaves aren't an easy shape to appliqué, though, so I have stolen the beautiful autumn leaves from our cherry trees for this dramatic modern quilt. I think this would make an amazing wallhanging or the perfect single bed quilt for a nature-loving child. It's also the quickest quilt top in the whole book and can be finished in a day if you decide to use raw edge appliqué. I, on the other hand, like to take my time, and so I hand stitched all the leaves.

MATERIALS

Assorted neutral prints (beige, gray, cream, taupe, and charcoal): 1½ yards total for tree trunks

Green print: 1⅔ yards for foreground

Turquoise print: 1⅞ yards for sky

Assorted orange and yellow prints: ¾ yard total for leaves

Binding: ⅝ yard

Backing (pieced crosswise): 3¾ yards

Batting: 63" × 80"

Patterns A and B (pages 122 and 124)

CUTTING

Assorted neutral prints

- Cut 2 strips 1" × 20".
- Cut 1 strip 1¼" × 20".
- Cut 6 strips 1½" × 20".
- Cut 8 strips 2" × 20".
- Cut 6 strips 2½" × 20".
- Cut 2 strips 3" × 20".
- Cut 1 strip 3¼" × 20".
- Cut 1 strip 3½" × 20".
- Cut 1 strip 4" × 20".
- Cut 2 strips 4½" × 20".
- Cut 1 strip 5" × 20".

Green print

- Cut 1 piece 16" × 57".

Turquoise print

- Cut 1 piece 63" × width of fabric; subcut:

  1 strip 7½" × 63"

  1 strip 6½" × 63"

  1 strip 4½" × 63"

  1 strip 3½" × 63"

  1 strip 19½" × 63" (The strip may be less than 19½" wide, depending on the remaining width of fabric.)

Assorted orange and yellow prints

- Cut 28 using pattern A.
- Cut 22 using pattern B.

Binding

- Cut 7 strips 2½" × width of fabric.

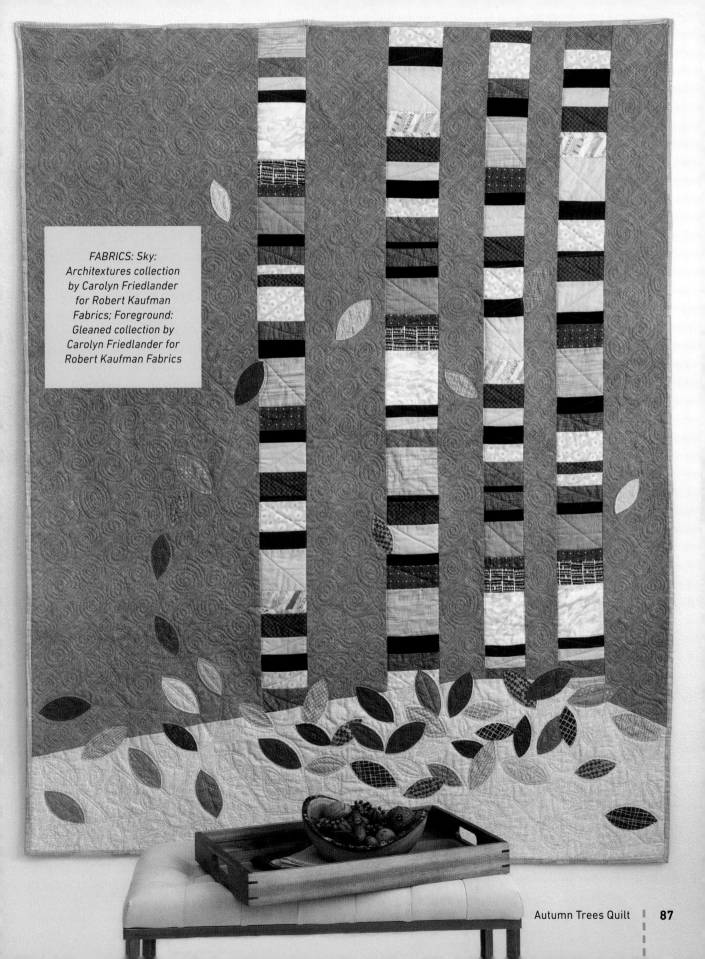

FABRICS: Sky: Architextures collection by Carolyn Friedlander for Robert Kaufman Fabrics; Foreground: Gleaned collection by Carolyn Friedlander for Robert Kaufman Fabrics

construction

Make the Tree Trunks

1. Sew together the 20″ neutral strips in the order shown to make 3 strip sets.

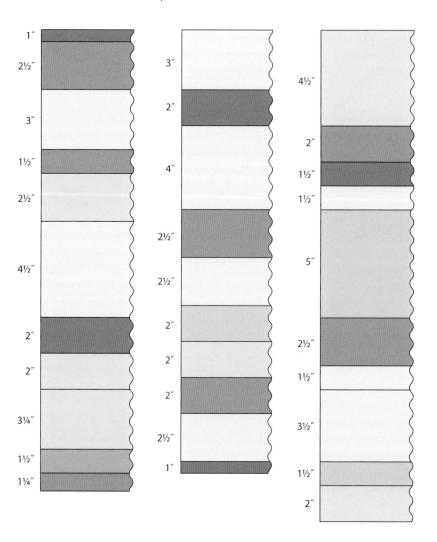

Strip set 1 (top to bottom): 1″, 2½″, 3″, 1½″, 2½″, 4½″, 2″, 2″, 3¼″, 1½″, 1¼″

Strip set 2 (top to bottom): 3″, 2″, 4″, 2½″, 2½″, 2″, 2″, 2″, 2½″, 1″

Strip set 3 (top to bottom): 4½″, 2″, 1½″, 1½″, 5″, 2½″, 1½″, 3½″, 1½″, 2″

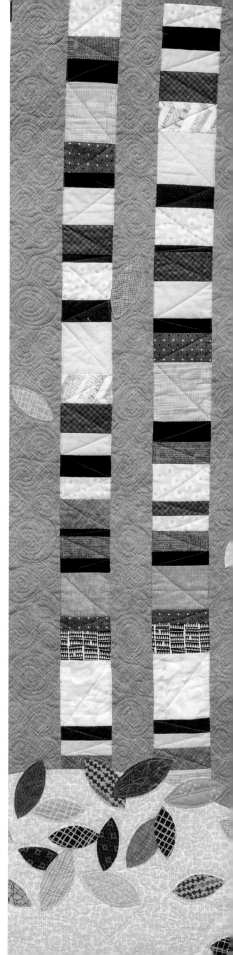

2. From each of these strip sets, cut the following sizes: 4″, 4½″, 4½″, and 5″.

3. Sew together the 3 strips measuring the same width. Sew the strips in a different order, turning some of them upside down for maximum variety. Make 4 different tree trunk pieces.

4. Sew the turquoise strips and the tree trunk pieces in the order shown, lining up the top edges (the bottom edges will be different lengths). Press well.

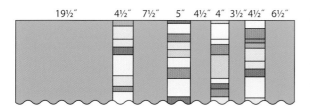

5. Using a large cutting mat, place the green print piece so that it overlaps the bottom of the tree/sky piece by around 8″, with both pieces right sides up. Using your rotary cutter, start at one edge and cut a slightly curving line (to create a slight hill in your landscape) through both layers across the whole width. If you prefer, you can draw this line first on the

foreground piece and use the cutter or scissors to cut on the line before placing it on top on top of the tree/sky piece and echoing the cut. Trim the green piece to match the sides of the tree/sky piece.

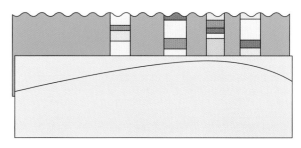

6. Flip the foreground piece over so that it is right sides together with the tree/sky piece. Starting in the center, carefully sew the curved seam toward one edge, gently easing as shown in Curved Piecing (page 74). Flip over, return to the center, and finish sewing the seam. Press.

Tip || **Freehand Curve Alternatives**

If that freehand curve is a little too scary for you to attempt, use your ruler to cut a slanting line for your hill, overlapping the fabrics with both right sides up as in Step 5. Or you can sew a perfectly straight edge to attach the foreground with no hill at all!

Add Leaves

Arrange the leaves in a pile on the foreground, tumbling from the sky and swirling upwards from the ground, and between and in front of the tree trunks. Pin to secure and use the turned-edge appliqué techniques (page 66) to stitch in place. Feel free to use the raw-edge techniques in the same chapter to attach your leaves. It's a good idea to place and sew a first batch of leaves and then add some more later to give the overlapping "pile of leaves" effect.

Finishing

Layer, quilt, and bind as desired. This quilt was finished by machine using both a free-motion quilting foot to create a pattern of leaves and spirals, and a walking foot to add diagonal lines to the trees.

Pinball Wizard Quilt

Finished block: 16″ × 16″
Finished quilt: 72½″ × 72½″

Using both your FPP and curved-piecing skills, you too can create this dynamic modern quilt design. Two of my favorite traditional patterns are Double Wedding Ring and Pickle Dish, and I have always wanted to combine them in the same quilt. As both patterns are quite tricky for a novice quilter, I have modified and simplified the blocks by using quarter-circles, strips, and HST units instead of the traditional lemon-shaped patterns. The design looks complex, but the blocks are actually very straightforward and you can use up some of those scraps you will have accumulated for the stripy curves. For the background, I have used a mixture of different low-volume fabrics: light neutral fabrics with just a hint of pattern. You could substitute a plain, light background fabric for this if you like. The whole thing reminds me of a psychedelic pinball arcade machine from the 1970s!

MATERIALS

Assorted low-volume prints:
3¼ yards total for background

Assorted solids and blender prints in a range of greens and turquoises: 2 yards total

Assorted solids and blender prints in a range of oranges:
1 yard total

Assorted solids and blender prints in a range of pinks:
1 yard total

Assorted solids in a range of purples: ½ yard total

Black print: ½ yard

Binding: ⅔ yard

Backing: 4½ yards

Batting: 80″ × 80″

Patterns A–E (pages 118–121)

CUTTING

Assorted low-volume prints

• Cut a total of 8 squares
  5″ × 5″.

• Cut a total of 28 outer curves using pattern D.

• Cut a total of 8 outer curves using pattern E.

• Cut a total of 8 strips
  4½″ × width of fabric for the border.

• Cut the remainder into
  5″ strips to use with FPP pattern B.

Green, turquoise, orange, pink, and purple solids and prints

• Cut a total of 40 strips
  2½″ × 4½″.

• Cut a total of 80 strips
  1½″ × 4½″.

Green and turquoise solids and prints

• Cut a total of 32 squares
  4½″ × 4½″.

• Cut a total of 8 squares 5″ × 5″.

• Cut the remainder into
  5″ strips to use with FPP pattern A.

Cutting continues on page 94.

Cutting continued

Orange solids and prints

- Cut a total of 16 squares 4½″ × 4½″.

- Cut a total of 16 inner curves using pattern C.

- Cut the remainder into 5″ strips to use with FPP pattern A.

Pink solids and prints

- Cut a total of 8 squares 4½″ × 4½″.

- Cut a total of 12 inner curves using pattern C.

- Cut the remainder into 5″ strips to use with FPP pattern A.

Purple solids

- Cut a total of 8 inner curves using pattern C.

- Cut the remainder into 5″ strips to use with FPP pattern A.

Black print

- Cut 3 strips 5″ × width of fabric to use with FPP pattern B.

Binding

- Cut 8 strips 2½″ × width of fabric.

tip || **Sharper Curves Ahead!**

As these curves are tighter than those for the Stream quilt, try practicing with some scrap fabric before using your prepared pieces.

----

construction

Block Assembly

Double Wedding Ring Blocks

Make 28 copies of FPP pattern A.

1. Following the FPP technique (page 79), piece pattern A using a mixture of prints. I used mainly greens and turquoises with just the odd pop of the other colors. Press and then trim the foundation pattern before removing the paper. Make 28.

tip || **Mix It Up!**

I mixed the colors up quite freely when piecing the FPP patterns and the squares, but I tended to keep the black and purple to use for the thinner strips. Have fun choosing the colors as you go along!

2. Using the curved-piecing technique (page 74), sew 1 orange C piece to 1 pattern A piece. Add 1 background D piece. Make 16 units.

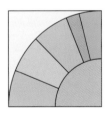

tip || **Piecing Tricky Curves**

Since the ends of pattern D are so tapered, you may find it easier to start sewing in the center and sew to the ends. Try it for the first few blocks.

3. Make the pieced squares by sewing 1 print rectangle 2½″ × 4½″ to 2 print rectangles 1½″ × 4½″ to make a square 4½″ × 4½″. You can place your pieces in any order you like and use a mixture of colors. Make 40 pieced squares.

4. Arrange and sew 2 pieced squares to 1 orange square 4½″ × 4½″ and 1 green/turquoise square 4½″ × 4½″. Note the seam placement of the pieced squares. Make 16 units.

5. Arrange and sew 2 curved A units from Step 2 to the 2 pieced square units from Step 4. Make 8 blocks for the quilt sides.

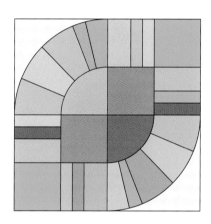

6. Using the curved-piecing technique (page 74), sew 1 pink C piece to 1 pattern A piece from Step 1. Add 1 background D piece. Make 12 units.

7. Arrange and sew 2 of the remaining pieced squares from Step 3 to 1 pink square 4½″ × 4½″ and 1 green/turquoise square 4½″ × 4½″. Make 4 units.

8. Arrange and sew the curved A units from Step 6 to the pieced square units from Step 7. Make 4 blocks for the quilt corners.

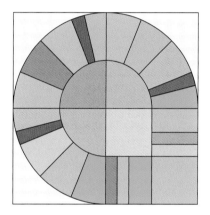

Pickle Dish Blocks

Print 8 copies of FPP pattern B.

1. Following the FPP technique (page 79), piece pattern B using a background fabric to cover the odd-numbered areas and the black print for the even-numbered areas (the spikes). Press and then trim the foundation pattern before removing the paper. Make 8 units.

2. Using the curved-piecing technique (page 74), sew 1 purple C piece to 1 pattern B unit. Add 1 background E piece. Make 8 units.

3. Following the 2-in-1 HST technique (page 48), make 16 HST units using 8 background and 8 green/turquoise squares 5″ × 5″. Press and then trim the units to 4½″ × 4½″.

4. Arrange and sew together 2 of the HST units to 2 green/turquoise squares 4½″ × 4½″. Press. Make 4 units.

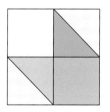

5. Arrange and sew 2 of the HST units to 1 green/turquoise square 4½″ × 4½″ and 1 pink square 4½″ × 4½″. Press. Make 4 units.

6. Arrange and sew the curved B units from Step 2 to the HST units from Steps 4 and 5. Make 4 blocks for the quilt center.

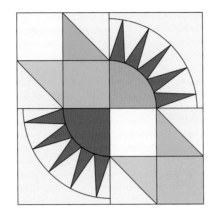

Quilt Construction

1. Arrange and sew together 4 rows of 4 blocks each. Press. Join the rows and press.

2. Cut the 8 background strips 4½″ × width of fabric into random lengths and sew into one long strip. From this strip, cut 2 strips 4½″ × 64½″ and 2 strips 4½″ × 72½″.

3. Pin and sew the 4½″ × 64½″ lengths to opposite sides of the top. Press. Sew the 4½″ × 72½″ lengths to the remaining sides. Press.

Quilt assembly

Finishing

Layer, quilt, and bind as desired. This quilt was finished by Tatyana Duffie on a longarm machine.

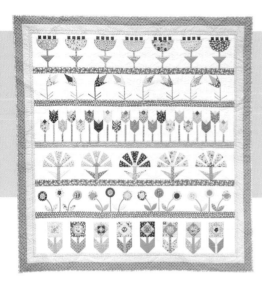

Bedding Plants Quilt

Finished blocks:

Poppy: 8″ × 10″ Fan Flower: 12″ × 10″

Crocus: 13½″ × 8″ Daisy: 16″ × 8″

Tulip units: 4″ × 4″ Rose: 4¾″ × 11″

Finished quilt:

75½″ × 80¼″

Let's combine all those skills and techniques we've learned together to create this garden-inspired row quilt! We'll be using appliqué, curved piecing, FPP, and triangles to create six different rows of flowers, all on a cream background. Using these vintage-style ditzy prints and coordinating solids makes this look scrappy and traditional while still retaining a fresh prettiness. When I was thinking of a name for a quilt that depicts rows of flowers, the name *Bedding Plants* popped into my head. This seemed like the perfect title for a quilt that will likely be used on a different type of bed and so satisfies my love of puns and word play!

MATERIALS

Cream solid: 4¾ yards for background

Vintage-style prints and coordinating solids: 28 fat quarters

Red solid: ⅛ yard

Assorted gray prints: 1 yard total for sashing

Yellow print: ⅜ yard for border

Blue print: ¾ yard for border

Green print: 1 yard for border

Binding: ¾ yard

Backing: 4¾ yards

Batting: 83″ × 87″

Patterns for Poppy, Crocus, Fan Flower, and Daisy blocks (pages 111–118, 122, 123, and 125)

FABRICS: Lemonade
Sundae collection by
Leonie Bateman and Mon
Beau Jardin collection
by Nadra Ridgeway, both
for Penny Rose Fabrics
(Riley Blake Designs)

CUTTING

Poppy (7 blocks)

Cream solid

- Cut 1 strip 1¾″ × width of fabric; subcut into 2 strips 1¾″ × 11″.

- Cut 3 strips 1″ × width of fabric; subcut into 3 strips 1″ × 11″ and 7 rectangles 1″ × 8½″.

- Cut 4 strips 2″ × width of fabric; subcut into 28 rectangles 2″ × 4¼″.

- Cut 1 strip 2¼″ × width of fabric; subcut into 14 rectangles 2¼″ × 2½″.

- Cut 1 strip 3″ × width of fabric; subcut into 7 squares 3″ × 3″.

- Cut 3 strips 1½″ × width of fabric; subcut into 8 rectangles 1½″ × 10½″.

- Cut 14 outer curves using pattern B.

Vintage-style prints and solids

- Cut 7 strips 1″ × 5½″ for the stems.

- Cut 7 squares 3″ × 3″ for the leaves.

- Cut 14 inner curve pieces using pattern A (2 each from 7 fabrics).

Red solid

- Cut 2 strips 1½″ × width of fabric; subcut into 4 strips 1½″ × 11″.

Crocus (4 blocks)

Cream solid

- Cut 3 strips 5″ × width of fabric for the FPP background.

- Cut 1 strip 2½″ × width of fabric; subcut into 8 rectangles 2½″ × 4½″.

- Cut 2 strips 2″ × width of fabric; subcut into 7 rectangles 2″ × 8½″.

- Cut 1 strip 3¼″ × width of fabric; subcut into 2 rectangles 3¼″ × 8½″.

Vintage-style prints and solids

- Cut 1 square 3¼″ × 3¼″ from 8 different fabrics for the FPP flower centers.

- Cut 1 piece 4″ × 5″ from 8 different fabrics for the FPP flowers.

- Cut 1 square 5″ × 5″ from 8 different fabrics for the FPP leaves and stems.

Tulips (21 blocks)

Cream solid

- Cut 2 strips 3″ × width of fabric; subcut into 21 squares 3″ × 3″.

- Cut 3 strips 1½″ × width of fabric; subcut into 21 squares 1½″ × 1½″ and 21 rectangles 1½″ × 2½″.

- Cut 2 strips 5″ × width of fabric; subcut into 16 squares 5″ × 5″.

- Cut 1 strip 4⅞″ × width of fabric; subcut 6 squares 4⅞″ × 4⅞″.

- Cut 1 square 6½″ × 6½″.

- Cut 1 strip 1½″ × width of fabric; subcut into 2 rectangles 1½″ × 11¼″.

Vintage-style prints and solids

- Cut 21 squares 3″ × 3″.

- Cut 21 squares 2½″ × 2½″ to match the squares 3″ × 3″.

- Cut 21 contrasting squares 1½″ × 1½″.

- Cut 16 rectangles 1″ × 7″ for the stems.

Fan Flower (5 blocks)

Cream solid

- Cut 1 strip 5″ × width of fabric for the FPP patterns A and B.

- Cut 2 strips 5″ × width of fabric for the FPP patterns D and E.

- Cut 10 outer curves using pattern C.

- Cut 1 strip 2½″ × width of fabric; subcut into 2 rectangles 2½″ × 10½″.

Vintage-style prints and solids

- Cut 5 different squares 3″ × 3″ for the FPP flower centers.

- Cut 1 piece 5″ × 16″ from 5 different fabrics for the FPP flowers.

- Cut 1 piece 2″ × 5″ from 5 different fabrics for the FPP stems.

- Cut 1 piece 4½″ × 5″ from 5 different fabrics for the FPP leaves.

Daisy (4 blocks)

Cream solid

- Cut 1 strip 17″ × width of fabric; subcut into 4 rectangles 9″ × 17″.

Vintage-style prints and solids

- Cut 12 using pattern A from 12 different fabrics.

- Cut 12 using pattern B from 12 different fabrics.

- Cut 16 using pattern C from 8 different fabrics.

- Cut 4 strips ¾″ × 5½″ from 4 different fabrics for the center stems.

- Cut 8 strips ¾″ × 5½″ on the bias grain of the same 4 fabrics for the outer stems.

Rose (8 blocks)

Cream solid

- Cut 2 strips 2½″ × width of fabric; subcut into 32 squares 2½″ × 2½″.

- Cut 1 strip 1¾″ × width of fabric; subcut into 8 rectangles 1¾″ × 5¼″.

- Cut 3 strips 3″ × width of fabric; subcut into 7 rectangles 3″ × 11½″.

- Cut 1 strip 4¾″ × width of fabric; subcut into 2 rectangles 4¾″ × 11½″.

Vintage-style prints and solids

- Cut 8 squares 2″ × 2″.

- Cut 16 squares 2¼″ × 2¼″. (Cut in groups of 2 of the same fabric.)

- Cut 16 squares 3″ × 3″. (Cut in groups of 2 of the same fabric.)

- Cut 16 squares 4¼″ × 4¼″. (Cut in groups of 2 of the same fabric.)

- Cut 16 rectangles 2½″ × 5½″ for the leaves.

- Cut 8 rectangles 1¼″ × 5½″ for the stems.

Assorted gray prints

- Cut 10 strips 2½″ × width of fabric.

Yellow print

- Cut 7 strips 1½″ × width of fabric.

Blue print

- Cut 8 strips 2½″ × width of fabric.

Green print

- Cut 9 strips 3″ × width of fabric.

Binding

- Cut 9 strips 2½″ × width of fabric.

construction

Block and Row Assembly

Poppy

1. Arrange and sew the cream strips 1″ × 11″ between the red strips 1½″ × 11″. Add the cream strips 1¾″ × 11″ to the ends. Press. Cut 7 segments 1½″ wide.

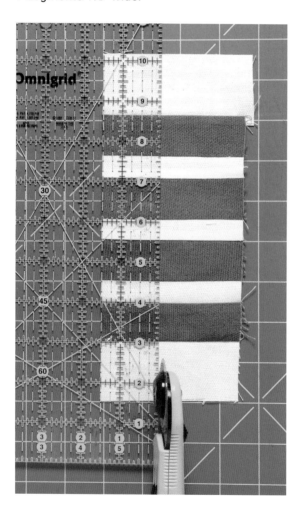

2. Using the curved-piecing method (page 74), sew 1 print A piece to a background B piece. Repeat with the matching print piece. Join. Make 7 units.

3. Sew a pieced segment from Step 1 to each top edge. Sew a cream rectangle 1″ × 8½″ to the top of the pieced segment. Trim the bottom edge ¼″ from the pieced curve. Make 7 blocks.

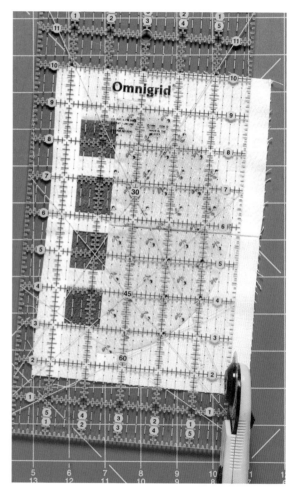

4. Using the 2-in-1 HST method (page 48) and the cream and leaf print squares 3″ × 3″, make 14 HST units. Trim to 2½″ × 2½″.

5. Arrange and sew the cream rectangles 2¼″ × 2½″ to the HST units. Add the cream rectangles 2″ × 4¼″. Sew to the print stem rectangle 1″ × 5½″. Press. Make 7 units.

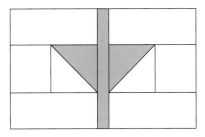

6. Arrange and sew the flower and leaf sections together. Press. Make 7 blocks.

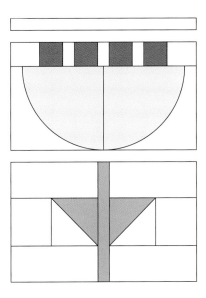

7. Sew the cream rectangles 1½″ × 10½″ between the blocks and at the ends of the row.

Crocus

Print 8 copies of FPP pattern A and 4 copies each of patterns B, C, D, and E.

1. Following the FPP technique (page 79), piece pattern A. Make 8 using different prints and solids.

2. Using the FPP technique, piece each pattern B and C with the same fabric. Sew together the B and C sections. Make 4 using different prints and solids.

3. Using the FPP technique, piece each pattern D and E with the same fabric. Sew together the D and E sections. Make 4 using different prints and solids.

4. Arrange pairs of the flower units from Step 1 so they face each other. Sew cream rectangles 2½″ × 4½″ to the outer edges of the flower units. Sew together with the B/C and D/E leaf-and-stem sections. Sew 4 cream rectangles 2″ × 8½″ between each pair to make 4 blocks.

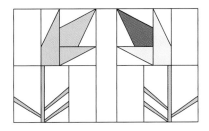

5. Sew 3 cream rectangles 2″ × 8½″ between the blocks. Sew 2 cream rectangles 3¼″ × 8½″ to the ends of the row.

Tulip

1. Using the 2-in-1 HST method (page 48), 21 cream squares 3″ × 3″, and 21 print/solid squares 3″ × 3″, make 42 HST units. Trim each to 2½″ × 2½″.

2. Arrange and sew 1 print/solid square 1½″ × 1½″ to 1 cream square 1½″ × 1½″. Sew together with 1 cream rectangle 1½″ × 2½″. Make 21 units.

3. Arrange and sew together 2 HST units, 1 matching print/solid square 2½″ × 2½″, and 1 unit from Step 2. Make 21 blocks.

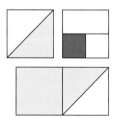

4. Cut 1 cream square 5″ × 5″ in half diagonally. Sew 1 stem rectangle 1″ × 7″ to the cut edges. Press. Trim the ends of the stem rectangle to true up. Make 16 units.

5. Trim 10 units from Step 4 to 4½″ × 4½″.

6. Cut 6 units from Step 4 in half diagonally, crossing the stem. Discard one triangle.

7. Cut the cream square 6½″ × 6½″ and the cream squares 4⅞″ × 4⅞″ in half diagonally. Discard one small triangle.

- -

8. Arrange and sew together the blocks, stem squares and triangles, and the small cream triangles in diagonal rows. Press. Join the rows. Add the large cream triangles and press. True up the edges as needed.

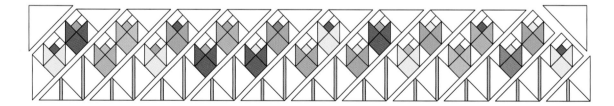

9. Sew 2 cream rectangles 1½″ × 11¼″ to the ends of the row.

Fan Flower

Print 5 copies each of FPP patterns A, B, D, and E.

1. Following the FPP technique (page 79), piece patterns A and B using matching fabrics. Make 5 of each pattern. Remove the paper.

2. Using the curved-piecing technique (page 74), sew a cream C piece to the curved edge of the A and B pieces. Sew the sections together. Make 5 units.

3. Using the FPP technique, piece patterns D and E. Sew the sections together. Make 5 units. Remove the paper.

4. Sew the flower units from Steps 1 and 2 to the leaf/stem units from Step 3. Make 5 blocks.

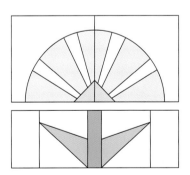

5. Arrange and sew together 5 blocks to make a row. Sew 2 cream rectangles 2½″ × 10½″ to the ends of the row.

Daisy

1. Trace or copy the daisy placement pattern onto paper. Trace the lines to the back of the paper using a lightbox. Trace the pattern onto one-half of the cream rectangles 9″ × 17″; then turn the pattern over to trace onto the other half of the rectangle.

2. Following the turned-edge appliqué instructions (page 66), stitch the stems and the pattern C leaves.

3. Using the card-and-foil method (page 67), prepare the circles using pattern A and stitch in place.

4. Using the paper method (page 66), prepare the circles using pattern B and stitch to the centers of the pattern A circles.

5. Make 4 blocks. Trim the blocks to 8½″ × 16½″.

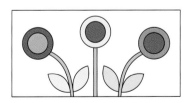

6. Sew together 4 blocks to make a row.

Rose

1. Cut 2 matching print/solid squares 2¼″ × 2¼″ in half diagonally to make 4 triangles. Center the long edge of a triangle right sides together on opposite sides of a print/solid square 2″ × 2″ so that the triangle points extend equally on the ends. Pin and sew. Press.

2. Repeat with the remaining triangles on the other sides of the square. Press.

3. Trim to 2¾″ × 2¾″. This will allow slightly more than ¼″ from the corners of the first square.

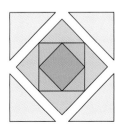

4. Cut 2 matching print/solid squares 3″ × 3″ in half diagonally. Sew to the sides of the unit from Step 3. Trim to 3¾″ × 3¾″. Again, this will allow slightly more than ¼″ from the corners of the previous square.

5. Cut 2 matching print/solid squares 4¼″ × 4¼″ in half diagonally. Sew to the sides of the unit from Step 4. Trim to 5¼″ × 5¼″. Make 8 units.

6. Mark a diagonal line on the wrong side of 2 cream squares 2½˝ × 2½˝. Place the squares right sides together on the ends of a print/solid leaf rectangle 2½˝ × 5½˝. Sew on the lines.

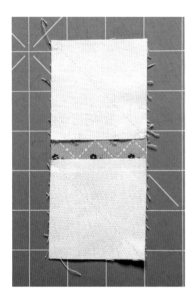

7. Trim the excess fabric ¼˝ from the line.

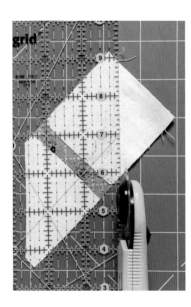

8. Open and press. Repeat to make 8 units.

9. Make another 8 leaf units following Steps 6–8, with the diagonal lines slanting in the opposite direction. Sew the print/solid stem rectangle 1¼˝ × 5½˝ between 2 leaf units.

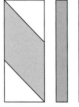 

10. Arrange and sew the flower and leaf units together, adding a cream rectangle 1¾˝ × 5¼˝ to the top. Make 8 blocks.

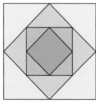

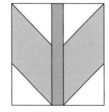

11. Sew cream rectangles 3˝ × 11½˝ between the blocks. Sew 2 cream rectangles 4¾˝ × 11½˝ to the ends of the row.

Quilt Construction

1. Arrange the flower rows as shown or as desired. Sew together in pairs the gray print sashing strips 2½˝ × width of fabric. From these, cut 5 strips measuring 2½˝ × 64½˝ each. Sew between the flower rows.

2. Sew together the yellow print strips 1½˝ × width of fabric to make one long strip. From this strip, cut 2 strips 1½˝ × 64½˝ for the top and bottom borders and 2 strips 1½˝ × 70¾˝ for the side borders.

3. Pin and sew the yellow top and bottom borders to the quilt top. Press. Pin and sew the yellow side borders to the quilt top. Press.

4. Sew together the blue print strips 2½˝ × width of fabric to make one long strip. From this strip, cut 2 strips 2½˝ × 66½˝ for the top and bottom borders and 2 strips 2½˝ × 74¾˝ for the side borders.

5. Pin and sew the blue top and bottom borders to the quilt top. Press. Sew the blue side borders to the quilt top. Press.

6. Sew together the green print strips 3″ × width of fabric to make one long strip. From this strip, cut 2 strips 3″ × 70½″ for the top and bottom borders and 2 strips 3″ × 79¾″ for the side borders.

7. Pin and sew the green top and bottom borders to the quilt top. Press. Pin and sew the green side borders to the quilt top. Press.

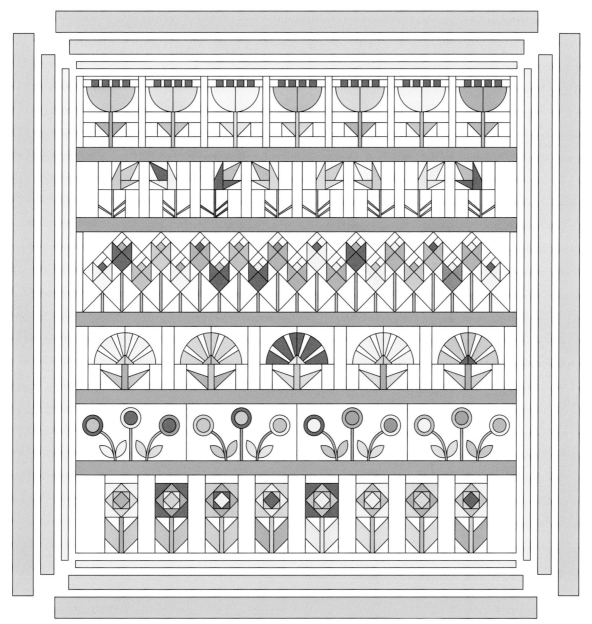

Quilt assembly

Finishing

Layer, quilt, and bind as desired. This quilt was finished by quilter Kelly Orr on a longarm machine.

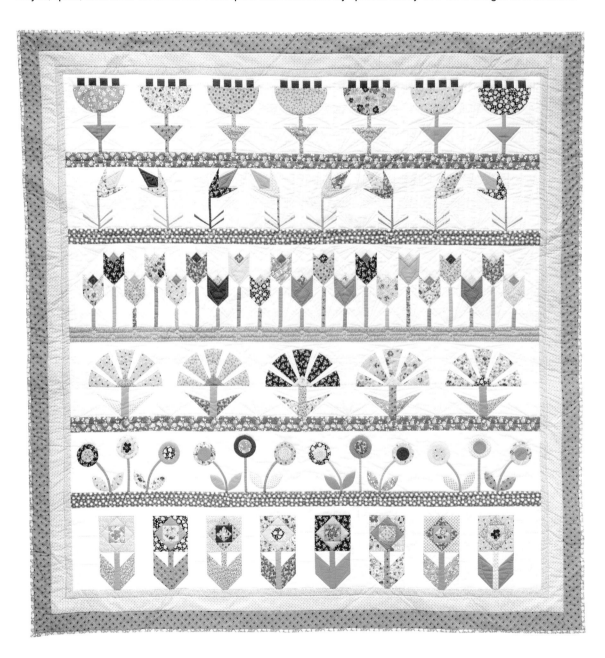

Patterns

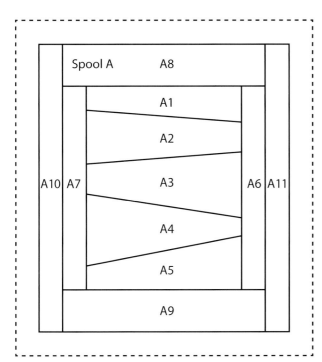

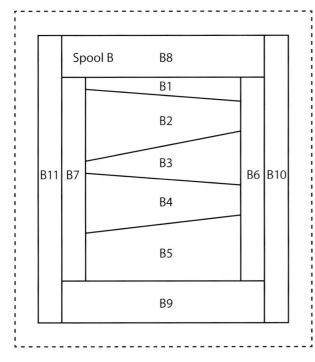

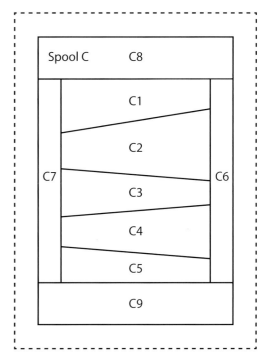

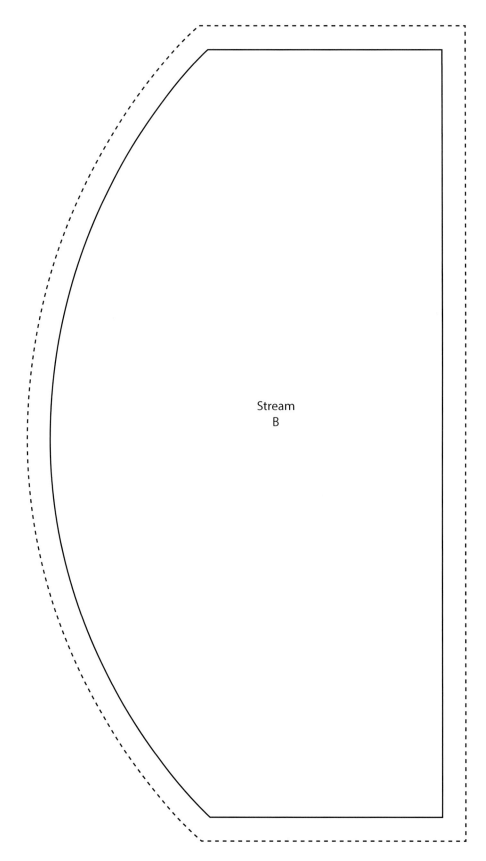

Stream
B

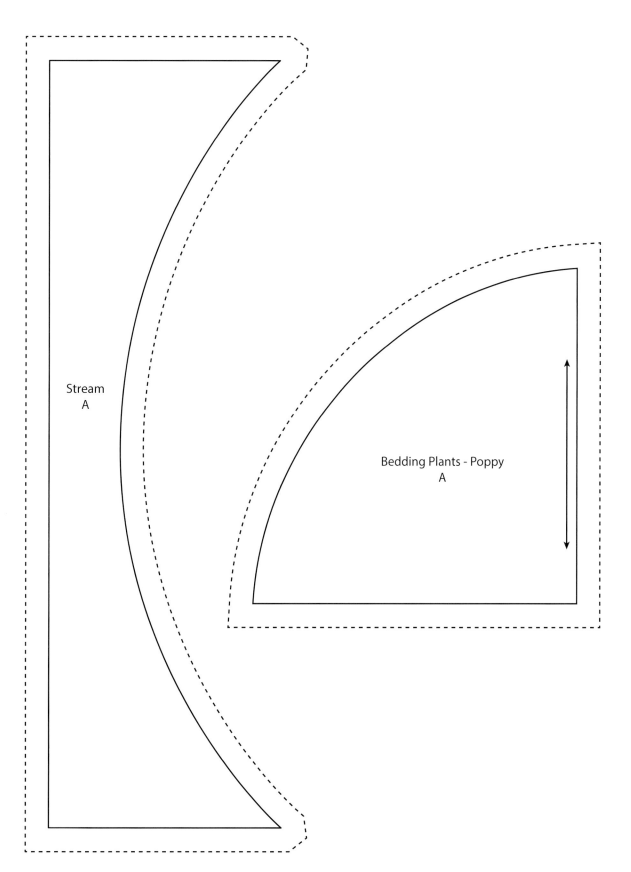

Stream
A

Bedding Plants - Poppy
A

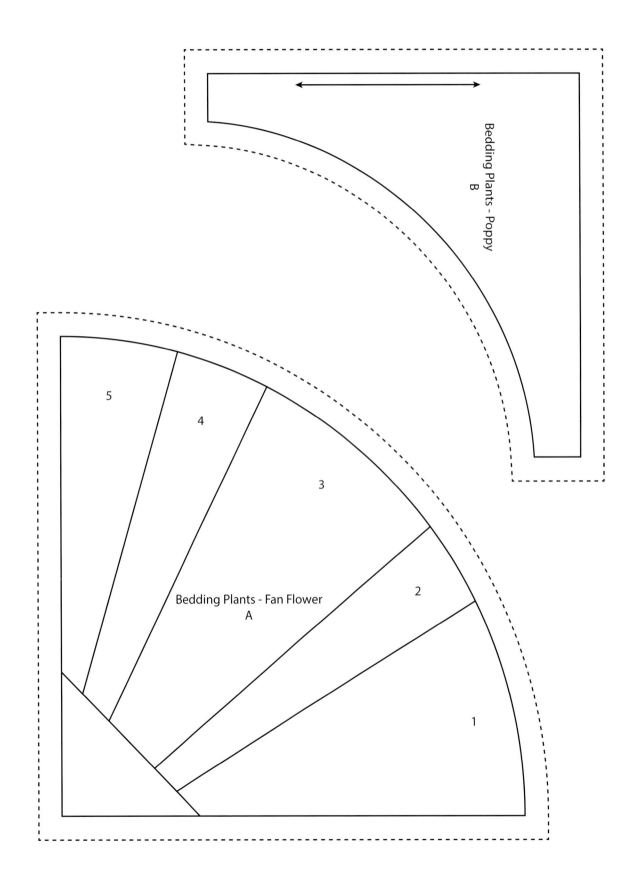

Bedding Plants - Poppy
B

Bedding Plants - Fan Flower
A

5

4

3

2

1

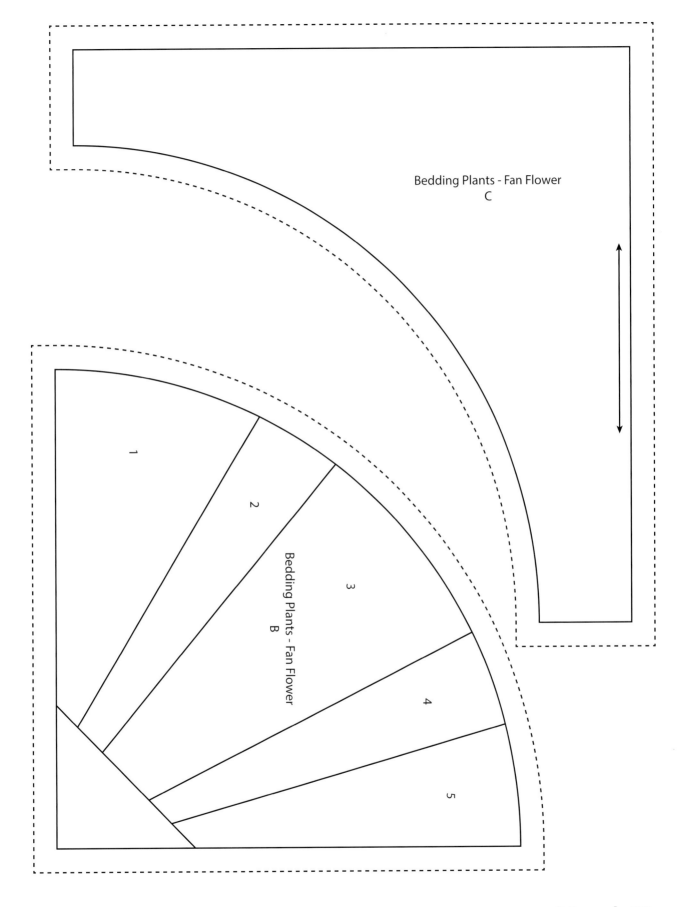

Bedding Plants - Fan Flower
C

Bedding Plants - Fan Flower
B

1
2
3
4
5

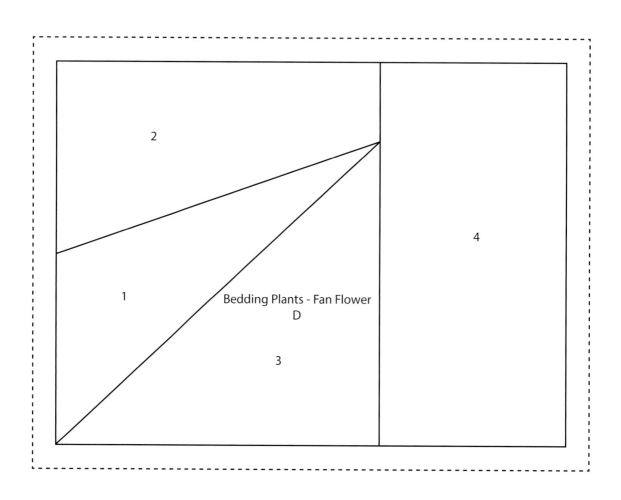

Bedding Plants - Fan Flower
D

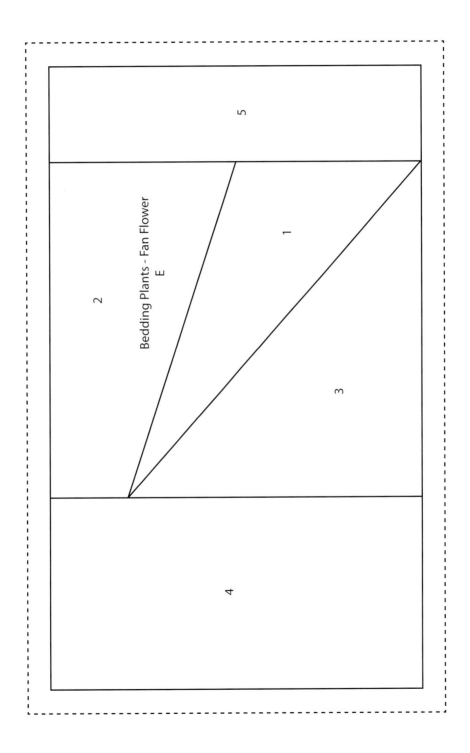

Bedding Plants - Fan Flower
E

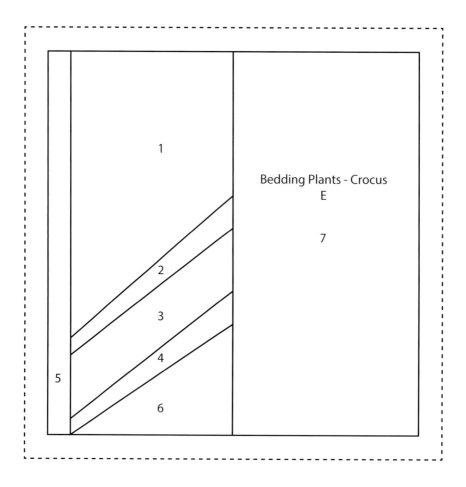

Bedding Plants - Crocus
E

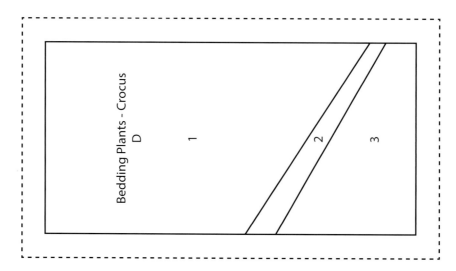

Bedding Plants - Crocus
D

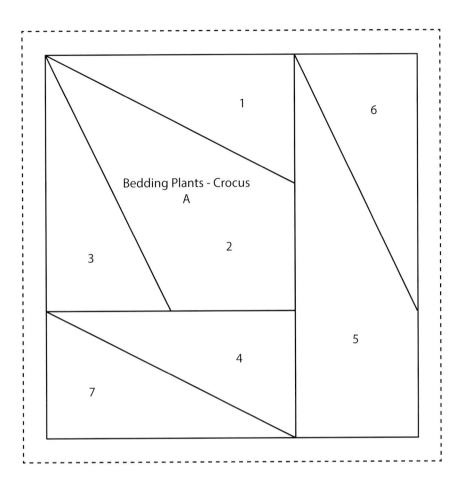

Bedding Plants - Crocus
A

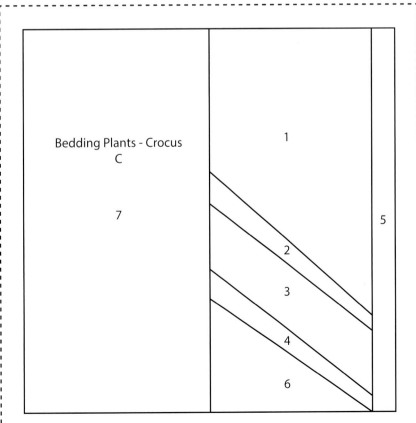

Bedding Plants - Crocus
C

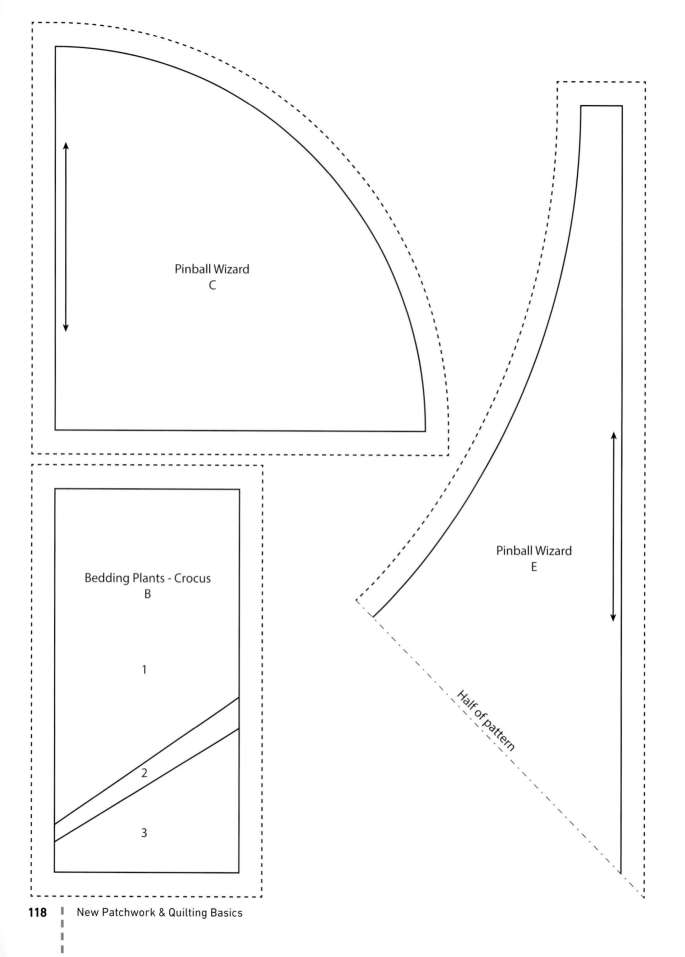

Pinball Wizard
C

Bedding Plants - Crocus
B

1

2

3

Pinball Wizard
E

Half of pattern

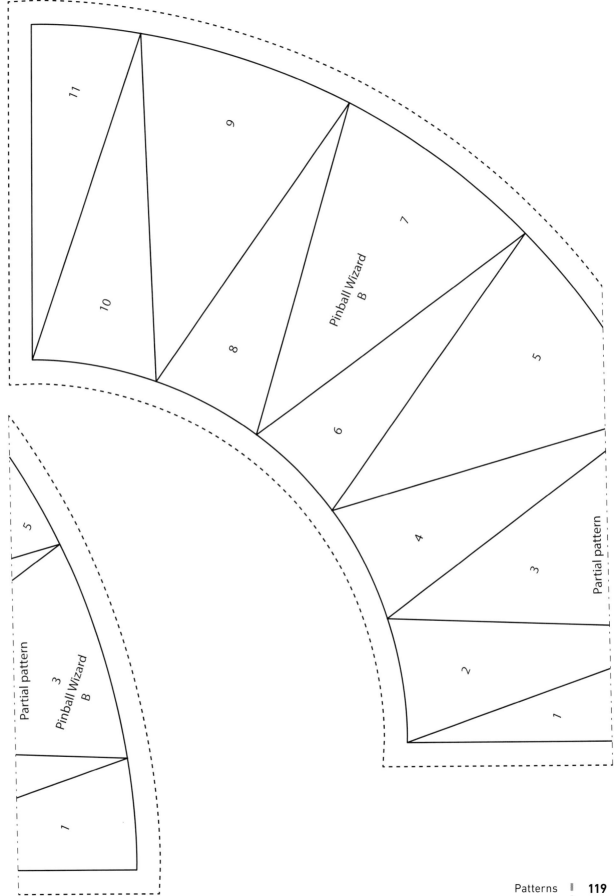

Partial pattern

11

9

10

8

Pinball Wizard
B

7

6

5

4

3

Partial pattern

2

1

Partial pattern

5

3
Pinball Wizard
B

1

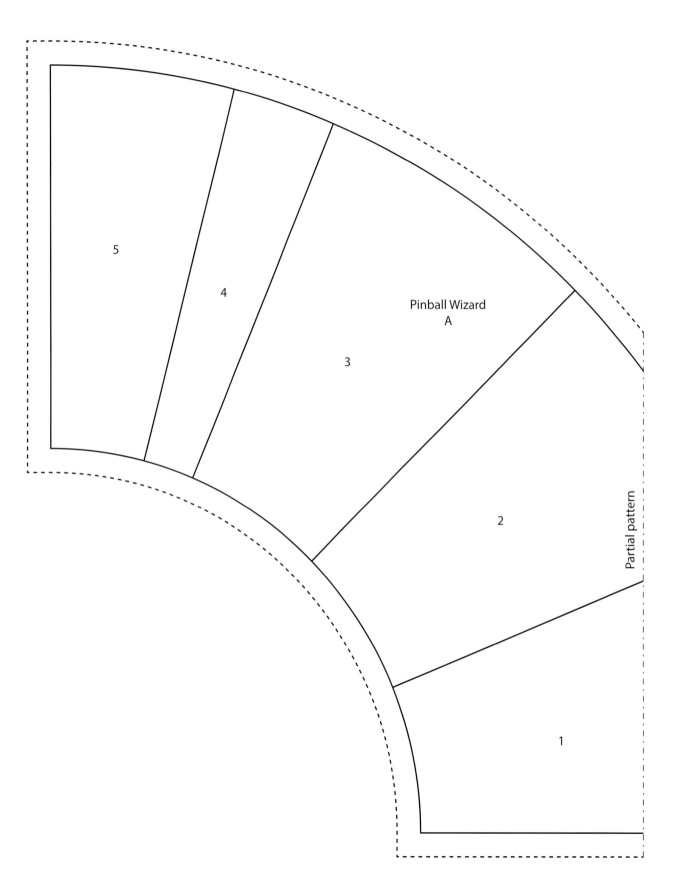

5

4

3

Pinball Wizard
A

2

Partial pattern

1

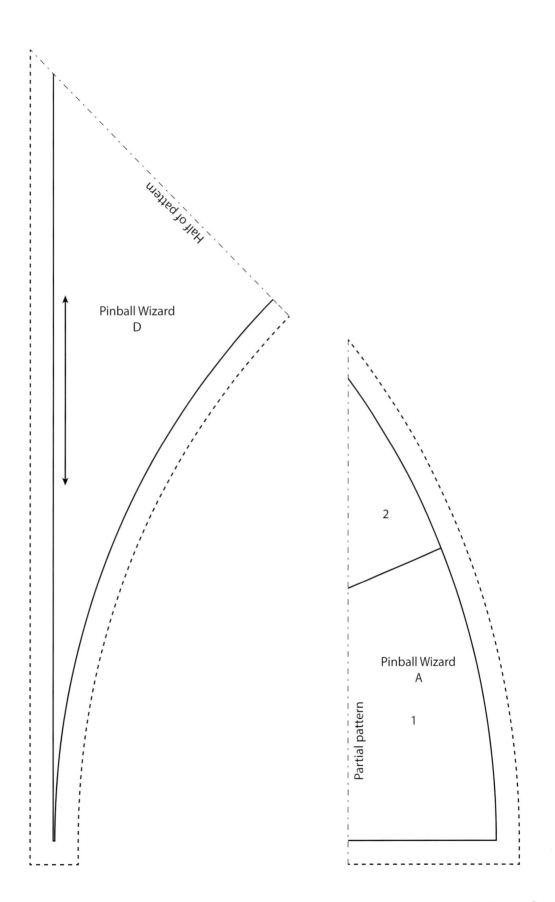

Half of pattern

Pinball Wizard
D

Pinball Wizard
A

2

1

Partial pattern

Flower Garland
Placement

Enlarge 125%.

Flower Garland
A

Autumn Trees
B

Bedding Plants
Daisy
C

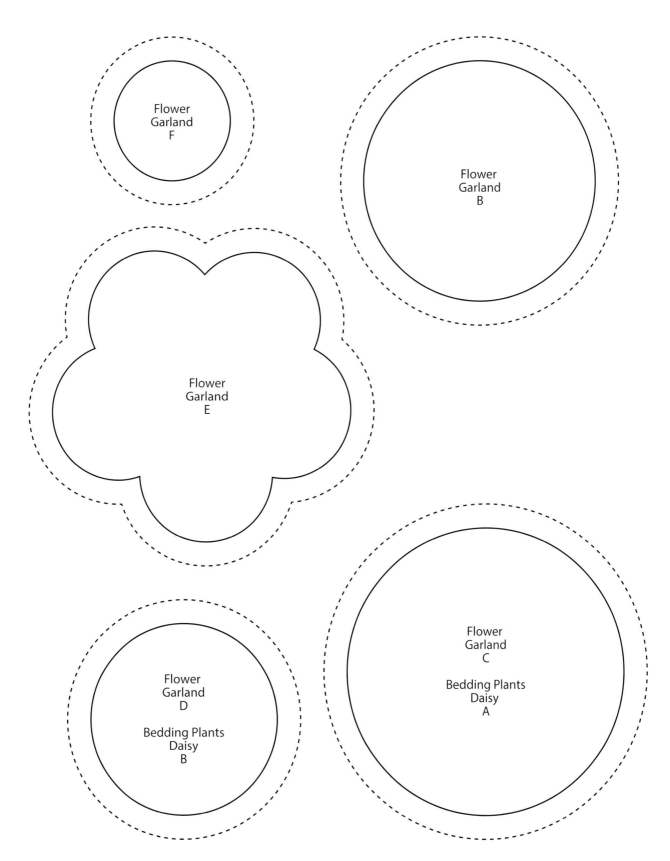

Flower
Garland
F

Flower
Garland
B

Flower
Garland
E

Flower
Garland
D

Bedding Plants
Daisy
B

Flower
Garland
C

Bedding Plants
Daisy
A

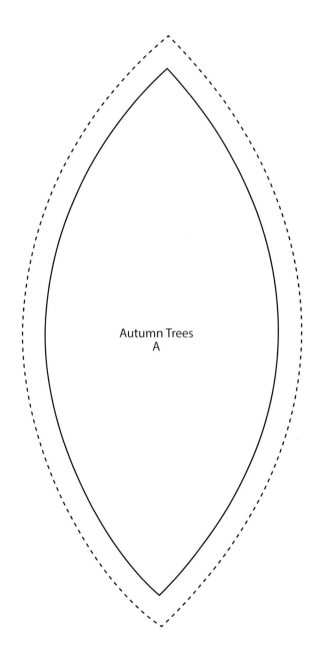

Autumn Trees
A

Half of pattern

Bedding Plants
Daisy placement

Photo by Jonathan Avery

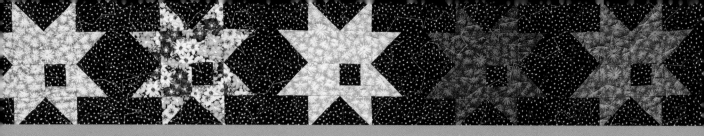

About the Author

Jo Avery lives in the countryside near Edinburgh in Scotland, surrounded by woodland and wildlife. She began her career in textiles and entrepreneurship at 21 years old with her first business, Cleopatra's Needle, which designed and produced needlepoint kits. Jo learned to make quilts soon after. She continued to pursue quilting as a hobby while bringing up a family and partnering with her husband, Jonathan Avery, in their furniture and retail business.

A decade ago, Jo discovered quilting blogs and began her own: *myBearpaw*. A whole new career of teaching crafts and designing quilt and embroidery patterns sprang from this. Jo now has her own teaching studio and fabric store in Edinburgh, teaches far and wide, designs quilts for a number of magazines, and organizes annual quilt retreats. *New Patchwork & Quilting Basics* is her first solo book.

Visit Jo online and follow on social media!

Website: mybearpaw.com

Facebook: /bearpawcraftclasses

Instagram: @mybearpaw

Want even more creative content?

Make it,
snap it,
share it
using
#ctpublishing